Our American Century

Hard Times · The 30s

By the Editors of Time-Life Books, Alexandria, Virginia

Contents

★

Too poor to ride, an Arkansas family walks through Texas to look for work in the Rio Grande cotton fields, a trek of about 900 miles.

Tavern patrons celebrate the repeal of Prohibition, December 1933.

Magazines on a Midwest newsstand in November 1938 mirror the joys and passions of a resurgent nation.

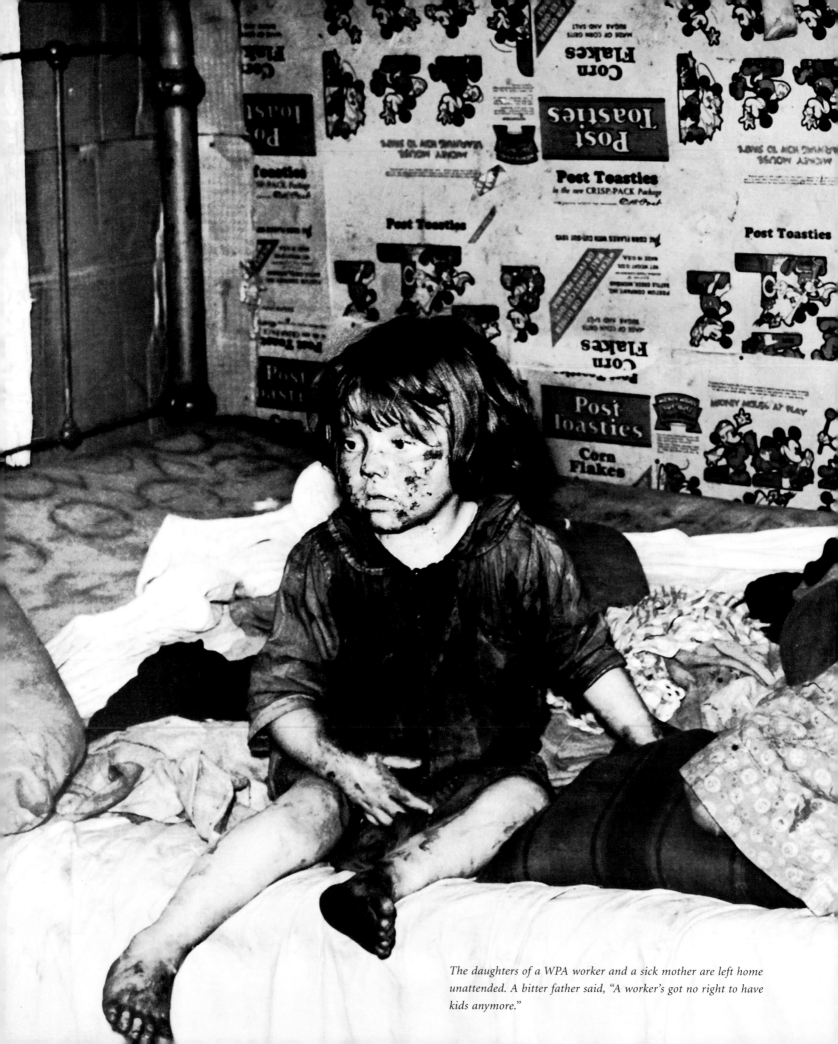

The daughters of a WPA worker and a sick mother are left home unattended. A bitter father said, "A worker's got no right to have kids anymore."

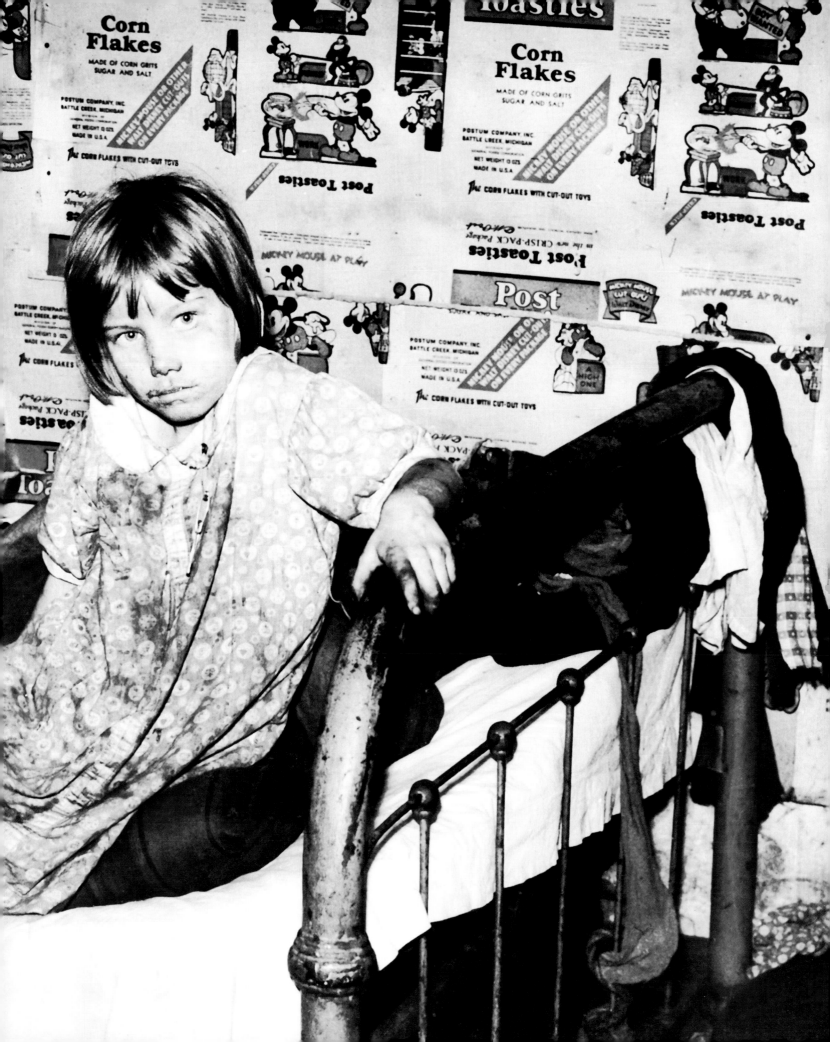

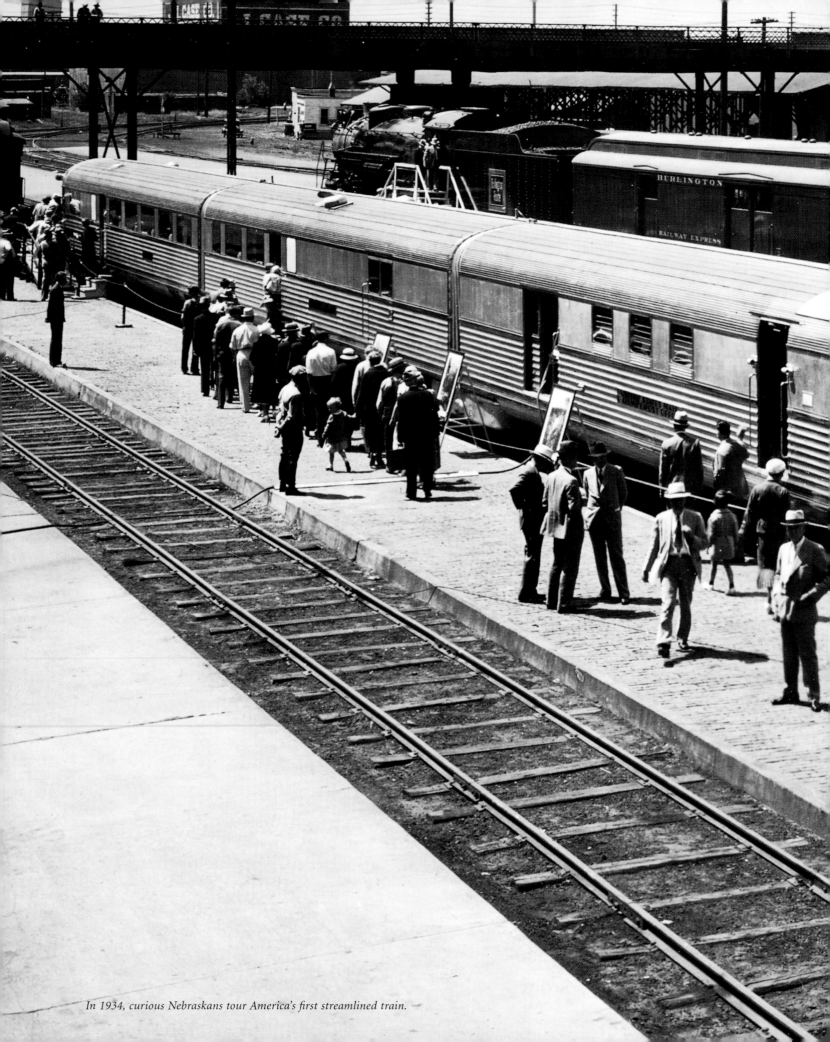

In 1934, curious Nebraskans tour America's first streamlined train.

Couples sway to the music during an afternoon dance at a Miami, Florida, trailer camp, 1938.

An intimate look into a
Hollywood bedroom suite
reveals how the other half
lived, about 1937.

Bathing beauties play in the sun in 1933 at Catalina Island, California.

A shopkeeper awaits his customers in New York's Bowery, 1935.

When You
BUY an AUTOMOBILE
You GIVE
3 Months' Work
to Someone

Which
Allows
Him to
BUY

OTHER PRODUCTS

BUY A CAR NOW—HELP BRING BACK PROSPERITY

Journey Through the Lean Years

Herbert Hoover stumbled out of bed at six o'clock on the chill, gray morning of March 4, 1933, to be told that on his last day as president the banking system of the United States had collapsed. The news was the final defeat in a disastrous term of office, and the weary president answered, "We are at the end of our string. There is nothing more we can do." His mournful words echoed the spirit of the nation and concluded the frantic but unavailing course it had taken under the outgoing president.

Not quite three and a half years had passed since the stock market crash had plunged the United States, and most of the world, into the worst economic debacle in Western memory. Industrial output was now less than half the 1929 figure. The number of unemployed, although difficult to count accurately, had mounted to something between 13 and 15 million, or a record high of 25 percent of the labor force—and the unemployed had 30 million mouths to feed besides their own. Hourly wages had dropped 60 percent since 1929, white-collar salaries 40 percent. Farmers were getting five cents a pound for cotton and less than 50 cents a bushel for wheat.

The stark statistics gave no real picture of the situation—of the pitiful men who sold apples on city street corners; of the long lines of haggard men and women who waited for dry bread or thin soup, meager sustenance dispensed by private and municipal charities; of the bloated bellies of starving children; of the distraught farmers blocking roads to dump milk cans in a desperate effort to force up the price of milk. "They say blockading the highway's illegal," said an Iowa farmer. "I says, 'Seems to me there was a Tea Party in Boston that was illegal too.'"

Everywhere there was hunger. "We saw a crowd of some 50 men fighting over a barrel of garbage which had been set outside the back door of a restaurant," said an observer in Chicago. "American citizens fighting for scraps of food like animals!" As though they had not troubles enough, millions of workless, hungry, and beaten people lacked even the constitutional right to vote. In September 1932 the city officials of Lewiston, Maine, voted to bar all welfare recipients from the polls; at least 10 states from Massachusetts to Oregon had poll tax and property

> ## "We are the first nation in the history of the world to go to the poorhouse in an automobile."
>
> Will Rogers

A poster (opposite) urged Americans to help the economy. "How'd they expect us to buy autos when we can't buy food?" a tinsmith asked.

Annual Earnings: 1932 to 1934

Airline pilot	$8,000.00
Airline stewardess	1,500.00
Apartment house superintendent	1,500.00
Bituminous coal miner	723.00
Bus driver	1,373.00
Chauffeur	624.00
Civil service employee	1,284.00
College teacher	3,111.00
Construction worker	907.00
Dentist	2,391.00
Department-store model	936.00
Doctor	3,382.00
Dressmaker	780.00
Electrical worker	1,559.00
Engineer	2,520.00
Fire chief (city of 30,000 to 50,000)	2,075.00
Hired farm hand	216.00
Housemother—boys' school	780.00
Lawyer	4,218.00
Live-in maid	260.00
Mayor (city of 30,000 to 50,000)	2,317.00
Pharmaceutical salesman	1,500.00
Police chief (city of 30,000 to 50,000)	2,636.00
Priest	831.00
Public-school teacher	1,227.00
Publicity agent	1,800.00
Railroad conductor	2,729.00
Railroad executive	5,064.00
Registered nurse	936.00
Secretary	1,040.00
Statistician	1,820.00
Steelworker	422.87
Stenographer-bookkeeper	936.00
Textile worker	435.00
Typist	624.00
United States congressman	8,663.00
Waitress	520.00

requirements beyond the reach of Depression victims; and a million or more nomads, wandering about the country, lacked the residency requirements for voting.

For all that, scores of the surviving rich and far too many of those in public office seemed blind to the miserable realities of the Depression. "I do not believe in any quick or spectacular remedies for the ills from which the world is suffering, nor do I share the belief that there is fundamentally anything wrong with the social system," said multimillionaire Andrew Mellon, former secretary of the treasury.

"There is something about too much prosperity that ruins the fiber of the people," said diplomat Dwight Morrow when he was running for governor of New Jersey. "People are growing more courteous in business, and often more reasonable at home, thoughtless women especially," editorialized the *Literary Digest,* adding, "Unappreciative wives who were indifferent to their husbands and neglected their homes have become tame and cautious." The Metropolitan Life Insurance Company had a grimmer observation. It reported that 20,000 persons committed suicide in 1931, a figure that far exceeded the legendary suicides of the months following the crash.

Hoover himself plugged away with firm-jawed righteousness that won him no thanks from the hopeless millions. "Economic depression cannot be cured by legislative action or executive pronouncement," he said. Anxiously seeking some other solution, he was at his desk from 8:30 in the morning till late at night, with 15 minutes off for lunch, drafting proposals, breaking dozens of pencil points in his urgency. He pumped two billion dollars into the banks and investment houses of Wall Street through the Reconstruction Finance Corporation. But what was that to the white-collar worker whose life savings had been wiped out in the failure of his local bank? He proposed the appropriation of money "for the purpose of seed and feed for animals" in the drought-stricken farm belt. But the farmer's children went hungry and Hoover denounced as a "dole" the granting of money and food to human beings. He spent hours on the telephone picking brains and seeking support for this idea and that, and called meeting after meeting of industrial and financial moguls. The latter habit moved the Baltimore *Evening Sun* to deride one such gathering as the president's "new panel of honorary pallbearers" and Representative George Huddleston of Alabama to growl, "In the White House we have a man more interested in the pocketbooks of the rich than in the bellies of the poor."

Hoover's stand against the concept of the "dole" was shared by thousands. But otherwise he was scorned and derided by most Americans, and his administration was so bitterly blamed for the Depression that his name became an adjective for all the manifestations of the blight.

There were "Hoover blankets," old newspapers used for warmth by park-bench tenants. Hoover flags were empty pocket linings turned inside out. In the country there were Hoover hogs, the jack rabbits that impoverished farmers caught for food, and Hoover wagons, broken-down cars restored to locomotion with the help of mules.

In cities all over the country there were "Hoovervilles" *(pages 40-41),* squalid villages that sprang up in the vacant lots where the homeless sheltered themselves in sheds made of packing boxes and scrap metal while they foraged about the city for food; New York had at least two Hoovervilles, one below Riverside Drive and the other in Central Park.

The biggest Hooverville of all sprang up on the president's doorstep in Washington, and from it emanated one of the sorest incidents of Hoover's luckless administration. Veterans of World War I had for some time been pleading for advance payment of a war bonus they were due to receive in 1945. In the spring of 1932 an unemployed Oregon canner, Walter W. Waters, conceived the idea of staging a sort of one-shot veterans' lobby in Congress. All through the month of June, war veterans and their families streamed into Washington, by freight car, by truck, and on foot, until they numbered 20,000.

The Bonus Expeditionary Force, as the veterans called themselves, found a hostile city; the only official

who made them welcome was Brigadier General Pelham D. Glassford, chief of the Washington police. He provided them with makeshift housing in empty government buildings, and when those ran out he allowed them to camp in a swampy area across the Potomac. He persuaded the army to lend them tents and cots, and rigged up an army field kitchen to provide them with food. He ordered his own men to treat them humanely, and he himself rode from site to site on a motorcycle, giving smiles and encouragement, calling the hopeful veterans "my boys."

Predictably, the Senate voted against the bonus, and most of the veterans left Washington to go home. But some 8,600 with no homes to go to stayed on in their Washington Hoovervilles, jarring the nerves of the president, who was by then engaged in a doomed campaign for reelection. Chains went up on the White House gates, guards patrolled the grounds night and day, and the streets were closed to traffic. On the morning of July 28, Glassford got word from the "highest authority" that the bonus marchers must quit the government buildings.

Glassford's cordial treatment of the men now stood him in good stead. He paid the veterans another visit and persuaded them to move out of their own accord, a request they set out to obey in return for his favors to them.

The evacuation proceeded all through the day, but the "highest authority" was not satisfied. Late in the afternoon General Douglas MacArthur, chief of staff of the United States Army, marched up Pennsylvania Avenue, with a major named Dwight D. Eisenhower at his side. They headed a parade of infantry, cavalry, machine guns, tanks, and trucks. That formidable array of weaponry, abetted by tear-gas bombs and sabers, scattered the few who remained. Not content with routing the squatters from the empty government buildings, the troops pursued fleeing women, children, and even a few legless veterans across the river to the swamp, where they burned the shacks that had been home to the pitiful ragtags for more than a month. In the last burst of gas bombs at midnight, an 11-month-old baby reportedly died, and the remnants of the veterans' march joined the throngs of Americans whom the Depression had already turned into nomads.

"A challenge to the authority of the United States Government has been met," said Hoover. But the episode cost him dear. The marchers never forgave him; neither did hundreds of thousands of sympathizers, who helped to vote Hoover out of office three months later.

The following year a second veterans' army assembled in Washington. Though it too failed to get the bonus payment, it received a far gentler White House recognition, in the form of an appearance by Eleanor Roosevelt *(pages 108-109)*, the new president's wife, who walked among the men, listening to their songs and tasting their humble chow. Mrs. Roosevelt's visit was not only humanitarian, it was also excellent politics. "Hoover sent the Army," cried the second crop of bonus marchers. "Roosevelt sent his wife."

That shrewd combination of practical politics and instinct for the common touch was to be the hallmark of the new administration, the one that was to leave its stamp on the nation and its government as the hard-times generation climbed out of the Depression. During the first 100 days of the new administration, Roosevelt's own sure-handed brand of personal leadership *(pages 98-115)* stirred the country out of its apathy and into effective action. In scarcely three months' time the government gave $500 million for cash, food, and shelter to the destitute, for the first time providing federal money for relief (the feared "dole") at the very bottom of the economic ladder. A series of other programs drawn up during this same period put the government squarely into the business of economic planning on a national scale.

Roosevelt called his startling array of legislation a "New Deal" for the nation. And indeed it seemed to be. The Federal Reserve Board's index of industrial production shot up from 59 in March 1933, the month that

Roosevelt took office, to 66 in April, 78 in May, 91 in June, and 100 in July, just 25 points short of the 125 high registered in the boom year of 1929. When in 1936 Roosevelt campaigned across the country for reelection, he looked out over the crowds that massed to meet him, flashed his brilliant, confident smile, and said with the air of a friend, "You look much better than you did four years ago," and the people cried in answer, "God bless you, Mr. President!"

Despite a business setback in 1937-1938, by 1939 the gross national product had climbed to $91 billion, an increase of more than 60 percent over the black days of 1933. As one bright promise of new prosperity, in October 1939 the DuPont Company put on sale in Wilmington 4,000 pairs of stockings made of a new fabric called nylon. It was the first fully synthetic fiber and represented an endeavor of such potential that even in the Depression DuPont was willing to spend $27 million developing it. Some wag claimed that the odd name for the new creation was an acronym made up from the words "Now You Lousy Old Nipponese," a slap at the increasingly unpopular nation of Japan, which bred the silkworms for the silk stockings that nylon would soon make obsolete. The new fabric was also a herald of dozens of wonder products that would someday be spread before millions of Americans— lightweight metal alloys, TV, synthetic detergents, and frozen foods. But most Americans would have to wait to make regular use of these new inventions, for the decade that had opened with the reverberations of the financial crash was to close to the rumble of distant gunfire. In 1939 German tanks rolled into Poland; England and France declared war on Germany; and before the decade was out, the United States was tooling up for its own defense. But through the travail of the Depression that lay between the two landmarks of the crash and the Second World War, America had managed to keep its political balance, regain its economic health, and reassess some of the old habits and values that had helped to lead it to the brink of these embracing cataclysms.

Depression Shopping List: 1932 to 1943

Automobiles

New

Pontiac coupe	$585.00
Chrysler sedan	995.00
Dodge	595.00
Studebaker	840.00
Packard	2,150.00
Chevrolet half-ton pickup truck	650.00

Used

Lincoln '27	125.00
Studebaker '30	200.00
Ford '29	57.50

Clothing

Women's

Mink coat	$585.00
Leopard coat	92.00
Cloth coat	6.98
Raincoat	2.69
Wool dress	1.95
Wool suit	3.98
Wool sweater	1.69
Silk stockings	.69
Leather shoes	1.79
Reptile-leather shoes	6.00

Men's

Overcoat	11.00
Wool suit	10.50
Trousers	2.00
Shirt	.47
Pullover sweater	1.95
Silk necktie	.55
Suede hunting shirt	2.94
Calfskin riding boots	9.50
Golf suit	20.00
Tuxedo	25.00
Stetson hat	5.00
Shoes	3.85

Household Items

Silver-plate flatware, 26-piece	$4.98
Double-bed sheets	.67
Bath towel	.24
Wool blanket	1.00
Linen tablecloth	1.00
Wool rug (9' x 12')	5.85

Appliances

Electric iron	$2.00
Electric coffee percolator	1.39
Electric mixer	9.95
Vacuum cleaner	18.75
Electric washing machine	47.95
Gas stove	23.95
Electric portable sewing machine	24.95
Copper lamp	1.95

Furniture

Dining-room set, 8-piece	$46.50
Bedroom set, 3-piece	49.95
Lounge chair	19.95
Double bed and spring mattress	14.95
Bridge table	1.00
Colonial walnut secretary	54.00
Mahogany coffee table	10.75
Chippendale mahogany sofa	135.00
Louis XV walnut dining table	124.00
Wing chair	39.00
Grand piano	395.00

Miscellaneous

Dental filling	$1.00
Toothpaste (large)	.25
Coty face powder	1.50
L'Aimant perfume (¼ oz.)	1.00
Cultivated Oriental pearls	35.00
Razor blades (10)	.49
Cigarettes	.15
Cigarette lighter	.39
Pipe	.83
Alarm clock	2.00
Fountain pen	1.00
Briefcase	1.00
Console radio	49.95
Electric shaver	15.00
Desk typewriter	19.75
Movie camera, 8 mm	29.50
Kodak Box Brownie	2.50
Automobile tire	6.20
Gasoline (per gallon)	.18

Toys

Doll carriage	$4.98
Sled	1.45
Tricycle	3.98
Two-wheeled bike	10.95
Fielder's glove and ball	1.25
Catcher's mitt	1.19
Leather basketball	1.00
BB air rifle	.79

Food

Sirloin steak (per lb.)	$0.29
Round steak (per lb.)	.26
Rib roast (per lb.)	.22
Bacon (per lb.)	.22
Ham (per lb.)	.31
Leg of lamb (per lb.)	.22
Chicken (per lb.)	.22
Pork chops (per lb.)	.20
Salmon (16-oz. can)	.19
Milk (per qt.)	.10
Butter (per lb.)	.28
Margarine (per lb.)	.13
Eggs (per doz.)	.29
Cheese (per lb.)	.24
Bread (20-oz. loaf)	.05
Coffee (per lb.)	.26
Sugar (per lb.)	.05
Rice (per lb.)	.06
Potatoes (per lb.)	.02
Tomatoes (16-oz. can)	.09
Oranges (per doz.)	.27
Bananas (per lb.)	.07
Onions (per lb.)	.03
Cornflakes (8-oz. package)	.08

Real Estate

Modern house, 6 rooms, 2-car garage, Detroit	$2,800.00
English cottage, 8 rooms, 3 baths, 1 ballroom, Seattle	4,250.00
Italian villa, 12 rooms, Westchester, N.Y.	17,000.00
Spanish stucco, 7 rooms, Beverly Hills	5,000.00

Travel

Air

New York to Chicago, round trip	$86.31
Chicago to Los Angeles, round trip	207.00

Rail

Chicago to San Francisco, round trip, 16 days in San Francisco	80.50
New York City to Scarsdale, N.Y., monthly commuter ticket	10.39

Sea

Tour of Europe, 60 days, 11 countries	495.00
Bermuda-Havana-Nassau cruise, 10 days	110.00
Around the world, 85 days, 14 countries	749.00
San Francisco to Hawaii, round trip	220.00
New York to California via Panama Canal	120.00

The cast of Gangbusters blasts away to open a new episode.

On the Air

Every weekday from 7:00 to 7:15 p.m., telephone use dropped 50 percent, car thieves had an easy time on empty streets, and many movie theaters shut off their projectors to pipe in pure radio while 30 million Americans—including President Roosevelt—tuned in to *Amos 'n' Andy.* Such devotion to a comedy serial—created in black-voice by white vaudevillians, Freeman Gosden and Charles Correll—was typical of radio audiences in the '30s. The big box in the living room was everybody's ticket to adventure, laughter, sweet music, and romance.

People listened for the openers of their favorite shows the way little children listened for the sound of a parent's car in the driveway. Starting after breakfast each morning, serial dramas kept listeners intrigued all day: "Can this girl from a mining town in the West find happiness as the wife of a wealthy and titled Englishman?" the announcer asked at the beginning of *Our Gal Sunday.* Everyone hoped so but no one knew for sure.

During supper the family listened to the news, and then sat back to a marvelous, manufactured world in which you supplied the pictures while the radio brought in the sound. Millions of meek citizens joined the cops to patrol the dangerous streets of *Gangbusters.* Folksy types eased down in their armchairs when Kate Smith *(opposite)* belted out her theme song, "When the Moon Comes Over the Mountain." And comedy fans giggled at Edgar Bergen and Charlie McCarthy *(page 37).* Never mind that Charlie was a ventriloquist's dummy. He seemed so real that the king of Sweden, Winston Churchill, and Hollywood's Louis B. Mayer all extended their hands to him upon being introduced.

Real drama came into homes, too. Radio reporters put their shiny microphones before the lips of newsmakers and let listeners hear Lou Gehrig when the great ballplayer, dying of amyotrophic lateral sclerosis, said at Yankee Stadium, "I consider myself the luckiest man on the face of the earth." Other tears fell when Edward VIII of England renounced his throne for the Baltimore divorcée Wally Simpson, "the woman I love." Americans stayed glued to their radios while commentator H. V. Kaltenborn told of the dying days of peace in Europe *(page 36).* But when actor Orson Welles simulated a news broadcast of a fictional invasion by creatures from Mars *(pages 38-39),* thousands of Americans poured into the streets in panic, sure the end of the world had come.

"There are three things which I shall never forget about America— the Rocky Mountains, the Statue of Liberty and Amos 'n' Andy."

George Bernard Shaw, 1933

Kate Smith, the "Songbird of the South," with her cheery "Hello everybody!" was heard by some 16 million fans every Thursday at eight.

Highlights of the Six-Day Week

As this schedule for the week of June 5, 1938, indicates, the big evening shows of radio's week ran from Sunday through Friday on four networks. (Two belonged to NBC and were code-named Red and Blue.) Saturday night most people went to the movies; a few stayed home to hear Your Hit Parade.

Sunday

7:00	JELL-O PROGRAM: Jack Benny, Mary Livingstone, Kenny Baker, Don Wilson, Andy Devine, Phil Harris's orchestra (NBC-Red)
7:30	BAKERS' BROADCAST: Feg Murray, Harriet Hilliard, Ozzie Nelson's orchestra (NBC-Blue)
8:00	CHASE AND SANBORN PROGRAM: Don Ameche, Edgar Bergen, John Carter, Dorothy Lamour, Stroud Twins, Armbruster's orchestra (NBC-Red)
8:30	CHARIOTEERS (MBS)
8:45	NEWS TESTERS: Leonard M. Leonard (MBS)
9:00	HOLLYWOOD PLAYHOUSE: Tyrone Power, guests (NBC-Blue)
9:30	JERGENS PROGRAM: Walter Winchell, news commentator (NBC-Blue)
10:00	HOUR OF CHARM: Phil Spitalny's all-girl orchestra (NBC-Red)
10:30	HEADLINES AND BYLINES: H. V. Kaltenborn, Bob Trout, Erwin Canham: news commentators (CBS)
11:00	DANCE MUSIC (NBC-Red)

Ozzie Nelson and Harriet Hilliard

Monday

7:00	AMOS 'N' ANDY: sketch (NBC-Red)
7:00	FULTON LEWIS JR.: Washington news commentator (MBS)
7:30	EDDIE CANTOR'S CAMEL CARAVAN: Benny Goodman's Quartet, Bert Gordon, Walter King, Fairchild's orchestra (CBS)
8:00	BURNS AND ALLEN: Tony Martin, Garber's orchestra (NBC-Red)
8:30	PICK AND PAT: comedy and music (CBS)
9:00	LUX RADIO THEATRE: Cecil B. DeMille, guests, drama (CBS)
9:30	TALES OF GREAT RIVERS (NBC-Red)
10:00	MAGNOLIA BLOSSOMS: Fisk Jubilee Choir (NBC-Blue)
10:30	FOR MEN ONLY (NBC-Red)
11:00	NETWORK SIGN OFF (Local programming only)

George Burns and Gracie Allen

Tuesday

7:00	AMOS 'N' ANDY: sketch (NBC-Red)
7:30	HEADLINES: news dramatization (MBS)
8:00	BIG TOWN: Edward G. Robinson, Claire Trevor, dramatization (CBS)
8:30	INFORMATION PLEASE: Clifton Fadiman, John Erskine, John Kiernan and others (NBC-Blue)
8:30	AL JOLSON: Martha Raye, Parkyakarkus, Victor Young's orchestra, guests (CBS)
8:30	THE GREEN HORNET: dramatization (MBS)
9:00	HORACE HEIDT AND HIS ALEMITE BRIGADIERS: Lysbeth Hughes, Yvonne King (NBC-Blue)
9:30	FIBBER MCGEE AND MOLLY: Jim Jordan, Clark Dennis, Betty Winkler, Mills's orchestra (NBC-Red)
10:00	BELIEVE IT OR NOT: Robert L. Ripley, Rolfe's orchestra (NBC-Red)
10:45	DALE CARNEGIE: How to Win Friends and Influence People (NBC-Red)
11:00	DEVELOPMENT OF MUSIC (MBS)

Fibber McGee and Molly

Wednesday

7:00	AMOS 'N' ANDY: sketch (NBC-Red)
7:30	ROSE MARIE: song stylist (NBC-Blue)
8:00	CAVALCADE OF AMERICA: guests, Voorhees's orchestra (CBS)
8:30	RALEIGH AND KOOL SHOW: Tommy Dorsey's orchestra, Edythe Wright, Jack Leonard, Paul Stewart (NBC-Red)
9:00	TOWN HALL TONIGHT: Fred Allen, Portland Hoffa, Van Steeden's orchestra (NBC-Red)
9:00	ANDRE KOSTELANETZ: Deems Taylor, guests (CBS)
9:30	BOSTON "POP" CONCERT (NBC-Blue)
10:00	KAY KYSER'S MUSICAL CLASS AND DANCE (NBC-Red)
10:00	GANGBUSTERS: crime dramatizations, Col. H. Norman Schwarzkopf (CBS)
10:30	MELODIES FROM THE SKY (MBS)
11:00	DANCE MUSIC (CBS)

Amos 'n' Andy

Thursday

7:00	AMOS 'N' ANDY: sketch (NBC-Red)
7:30	ST. LOUIS BLUES (CBS)
8:00	KATE SMITH: Ted Collins, Miller's orchestra (CBS)
8:30	THE GREEN HORNET: dramatization (MBS)
8:45	PIANO DUO (NBC-Blue)
9:00	MAJOR BOWES'S AMATEUR HOUR (CBS)
9:30	RAY SINATRA'S MOONLIGHT RHYTHMS: Sylvia Froos, Jack Arthur (MBS)
10:00	KRAFT MUSIC HALL: Bing Crosby, Bob Burns, Trotter's orchestra, guests (NBC-Red)
10:30	AMERICANS AT WORK (CBS)
11:00	SPORTS QUESTION BOX (NBC-Red)
11:00	DUKE ELLINGTON'S ORCHESTRA (CBS)

Jack Benny and Fred Allen

Friday

7:00	AMOS 'N' ANDY: sketch (NBC-Red)
7:30	TALES OF EDWIN C. HILL (NBC-Blue)
7:45	SCIENCE AND SOCIETY (CBS)
8:00	MAURICE SPITALNY'S ORCHESTRA (NBC-Blue)
8:30	DEATH VALLEY DAYS: dramatization (NBC-Blue)
9:00	HOLLYWOOD HOTEL: Louella Parsons, Frances Langford, Frank Parker, Ken Murray (CBS)
9:30	NBC SPELLING BEE: Paul Wing (NBC-Blue)
10:00	FIRST NIGHTER: dramatization, Les Tremayne, Barbara Luddy (NBC-Red)
10:30	JIMMIE FIDLER'S HOLLYWOOD GOSSIP (NBC-Red)
11:00	DANCE MUSIC (MBS)

War in Our Time

H. V. Kaltenborn stays with the microphone during a marathon newscast as assistants hand him the latest teletype reports of the Munich crisis.

H. V. Kaltenborn

Wednesday, 9:30 EST, CBS

Announcer: *H. V. Kaltenborn, dean of radio commentators . . . is going to tell you what he thinks about the headlines.*
Synopsis: *On September 14, 1938, with the world watching hopefully, Britain's Prime Minister Chamberlain left London to negotiate with Chancellor Adolf Hitler over the German claims on Czechoslovakia. During the 18 days of the crisis, Kaltenborn was on call to make his comments—such as those below—on the fast-breaking news.*

Kaltenborn: *[Chamberlain] is risking his prestige, risking his position, risking almost everything upon this journey. And the amazing thing to me, is that he's risking it now, before things have actually come to the point where war does seem inevitable.*

He has a plan—and perhaps that's the reason that he's going now. He has a plan that's been worked out between Britain and France. What can that plan be? Well, it can't be a plan for the immediate settlement of this problem. I don't believe that it would be possible to settle it as the result of a conversation between Cham-

berlain and Hitler alone. But, if the British follow the technique in which they are so adept and which they have used successfully in Spain and elsewhere, it will be a plan of postponement. The Czechoslovak delegate from Geneva said today: "Do we go on the butcher's block or have we found a champion who is going forth to battle?" Translated into other terms, that delegate is asking this: Must we Czechs give up to Germany our only dependable frontier, our richest industrial area and our right to exist as an independent nation? . . .

A great deal depends on the personal mood in which Hitler receives Chamberlain. Hitler is a man of moods. . . . I remember that when he invited me to Berchtesgaden he sent his private car with his chauffeur and the head of his Foreign Press service to Munich to meet me. I'm just wondering whether he's going to come to Munich himself to greet the Prime Minister of Britain.

If he does not, I think it will indicate he receives Chamberlain in the mood of a conqueror and that he considers that Chamberlain is coming to bargain. . . . I am convinced that Chamberlain will not go away empty-handed. He is bound to get something. . . . But my own feeling is that it will be little more than a truce. There is grave doubt as to whether or not the visit will bring peace.

Charlie McCarthy Meets His Match

In a battle of quips, comedian W. C. Fields (right) and Charlie McCarthy (left), the dummy of ventriloquist Edgar Bergen, trade wooden glances.

Chase and Sanborn Hour
Sunday, 8:00 EST, NBC

Announcer: *The makers of Chase and Sanborn Coffee—the blend of the world's choice coffees—now being sold at a very reasonable price—present Constance Bennett, Dorothy Lamour, W. C. Fields, Edgar Bergen and Charlie McCarthy, Ray Middleton, Werner Janssen and Don Ameche!*
Synopsis: *After chit-chat between actress Constance Bennett and Charlie, W. C. Fields, whom intimates call Bill, is introduced by announcer Don Ameche. Then:*

Bergen: *Excuse me, Don. Am I intruding?*
Ameche: *Frankly, Edgar, I'm glad you're here.*
Bergen: *I hope I didn't interrupt anything. . . .*
Fields: *Not at all Edwin . . . not at all. . . .*
Bergen: *Bill—I just came here to tell you something about Charlie.*
Fields: *I know enough about him already.*
Charlie: *Listen, Mr. Fields . . . I've got a bone to pick with you.*

Fields: *Yeah . . . Pick your head off.*
Charlie: *Aw gee whiz, Mr. Fields.*
Bergen: *You've got Charlie all upset, Bill. He's tried all sorts of ways to make friends with you.*
Charlie: *Yes. I've had people intercede for me . . . I brought you a bouquet of flowers. . . .*
Fields: *A nosegay! Go on!*
Charlie: *I don't know where to go or what to do.*
Fields: *I can tell you where to go and also what to do . . . If you want me to go into details.*
Charlie: *I don't know . . . no matter what I say, it seems to be the wrong thing.*
Fields: *Then sew a button on your lip.*
Bergen: *Now Bill . . . Charlie doesn't really feel good. Look how pale he is.*
Fields: *He needs a new coat of paint and a little furniture varnish. . . .*
Charlie: *This has gone far enough. I've been a little gentleman up to now. Mr. Fields . . . I'll clip you! So help me . . . I'll mow you down!*
Fields: *Go 'way—or I'll sic a woodpecker on you.*

Invasion From Mars

From the abundant schedule of radio programs, certain shows lingered in the minds of everyone who heard them. Among the most memorable was one that began as a Halloween joke but wound up scaring the nation half to death. On October 30, 1938, 23-year-old producer Orson Welles presented the radio play "Invasion from Mars," written by Howard Koch but mistakenly credited to H. G. Wells, from whose *War of the Worlds* the original idea had sprung. To make the fantasy seem credible the script simulated news broadcasts announcing that forces from Mars had landed in New Jersey and were devastating the countryside with death rays. The show was brilliant radio—and America panicked.

As Welles and his cast went through the script *(excerpted at right)*, thousands of people phoned their newspapers and local police to ask what they should do to avoid the invaders. In New Jersey, families tied wet cloths over their faces to escape "gas attack," piled into their cars, and clogged traffic for miles. A woman in Pittsburgh, screaming, "I'd rather die this way," was barely prevented from taking poison. At the end of the show, most listeners were apparently too frightened to hear Welles, chuckling, sign off by saying, "If your doorbell rings and nobody's there, that was no Martian . . . it's Halloween."

Belatedly realizing the commotion that the show had caused, CBS peppered the airwaves with reassurances that the play had been a spoof. But it took days before the last vestiges of terror had disappeared. How was it that so much of the nation went into shock at a Halloween joke? Explained one social scientist wryly, "All the intelligent people were listening to Charlie McCarthy."

Orson Welles narrated War of the Worlds on Halloween, 1938. Newspapers the next day reported a "tidal wave of terror that swept the nation."

Mercury Theatre on the Air

Sunday, 8:00 EST, CBS

Announcer: *The Columbia Broadcasting System and its affiliated stations present Orson Welles and the Mercury Theatre on the Air in War of the Worlds by H. G. Wells.*

Synopsis: *As the program opens, narrator Orson Welles explains, from an undetermined year in the future, that the smug people of the early 20th century did not know about the existence of "superior intelligences" on other planets. They learned, he says, on the evening of October 30, 1938, as they were listening to their radios.*

Announcer Two: *. . . We now return you to the music of Ramon Raquello, playing for you in the Meridian Room of the Park Plaza Hotel, situated in downtown New York. (Music plays for a few moments until piece ends . . . sound of applause)*

Now a tune that never loses favor, the ever-popular "Star Dust." Ramon Raquello and his orchestra . . . (Music)

Ladies and gentlemen, following on the news given in our bulletin a moment ago, the Government Meteorological Bureau has requested the large observatories of the country to keep an astronomical watch on any further disturbances occurring on the planet Mars. . . . Ladies and gentlemen, here is the latest bulletin from the Intercontinental Radio News. Toronto, Canada: Professor Morse of Macmillan University reports observing a total of three explosions on the planet Mars, between the hours of 7:45 p.m. and 9:20 p.m., eastern standard time. This confirms earlier reports received from American observatories. Now, nearer home, comes a special announcement from Trenton, New Jersey. It is reported that at 8:50 p.m. a huge, flaming object, believed to be a meteorite, fell on a farm in the neighborhood of Grovers Mill, New Jersey, twenty-two miles from Trenton. The flash in the sky was visible within a radius of several hundred miles and the noise of the impact was heard as far north as Elizabeth.

We have dispatched a special mobile unit to the scene, and will have our commentator, Mr. Phillips, give you a word description as soon as he reaches there. . . . We take you now to Grovers Mill, New Jersey. (Crowd noises . . . police sirens)

Phillips: *I wish I could convey the atmosphere . . . the background of this . . . fantastic scene. Hundreds of cars are parked in a field in back of us. Police are trying to rope off the roadway leading into the farm. But it's no use. They're breaking right through. Their headlights throw an enormous spot on the pit where the object's half-buried. Some of the more daring souls are venturing near the edge. Their silhouettes stand out. (Faint humming sound)*

One man wants to touch the thing . . . he's having an argument with a policeman. The policeman wins. . . . Now, ladies and gentlemen, there's something I haven't mentioned in all this excitement, but it's becoming more distinct. Perhaps you've caught it already on your radio. Listen: (Long pause) . . . Do you hear it? It's a curious humming sound that seems to come from inside the object. I'll move the microphone nearer. Here. (Pause) Now we're not more than twenty-five feet away. Can you hear it now? Oh, Professor Pierson!

Pierson: *Yes, Mr. Phillips?*

Phillips: *Can you tell us the meaning of that scraping noise inside the thing?*

Pierson: *Possibly the unequal cooling of its surface.*

Phillips: *Do you still think it's a meteor, Professor?*

Pierson: *I don't know what to think. The metal casing is definitely extra-terrestrial . . . not found on this earth. Friction with the earth's atmosphere usually tears holes in a meteorite. This thing is smooth and, as you can see, of cylindrical shape.*

Phillips: *Just a minute! Something's happening! Ladies and gentlemen, this is terrific! This end of the thing is beginning to flake off! The top is beginning to rotate like a screw! The thing must be hollow!*

Voices: *She's a movin'!*

Look, the darn thing's unscrewing!

Keep back, there! Keep back, I tell you.

Maybe there's men in it trying to escape!

It's red hot, they'll burn to a cinder!

Keep back there! Keep those idiots back!

(Suddenly the clanking sound of a huge piece of falling metal)

Voices: *She's off! The top's loose!*

Look out there! Stand back!

Phillips: *Ladies and gentlemen, this is the most terrifying thing I have ever witnessed. . . . Wait a minute! Someone's crawling out of the hollow top. Some one or . . . something. I can see peering out of that black hole two luminous disks . . . are they eyes? It might be a face. It might . . . (Shout of awe from the crowd)*

Good heavens, something's wriggling out of the shadow like a grey snake. Now it's another one, and another. They look like tentacles to me. There, I can see the thing's body. It's large as a bear and it glistens like wet leather. But that face. It . . . it's indescribable. I can hardly force myself to keep looking at it. The eyes are black and gleam like a serpent. The mouth is V-shaped with saliva dripping from its rimless lips that seem to quiver and pulsate. The monster or whatever it is can hardly move. It seems weighed down by . . . possibly gravity or something. The thing's raising up. The crowd falls back. They've seen enough. This is the most extraordinary experience. I can't find words. . . . I'm pulling this microphone with me as I talk. I'll have to stop the description until I've taken a new position. Hold on, will you please, I'll be back in a minute. (Fade into piano)

Hard Times

★

THE MISERY OF THE DEPRESSION

Shacks of Seattle's Hooverville shelter the homeless.

> **"I remember lying in bed one night and thinking. All at once I realized something. We were poor. Lord! It was weeks before I could get over that."**
>
> Depression victim, Chattanooga, Tennessee, 1933

Competition was stiff among the apple sellers in New York (opposite). Said one peddler, "People mostly hurry by as if they didn't want to look at you."

The Hungry Years

In 1930, before the full effect of the Depression was felt across the country, most Americans knew poverty only by reputation. But in the next several years, a large part of the richest nation on earth learned what it meant to be poor; for 40 million people poverty became a way of life.

Misery found its way into every region, group, and occupation. Black factory workers, always the last to be hired in good times, were the first to be fired as production slowed to a painful crawl. Farmers, struggling to keep on their feet amid plummeting crop prices, were knocked down for good by a series of natural disasters—floods, droughts, plagues, and dust storms. Businessmen slipped from being homeowners to room renters, and even to wandering the street. Experience taught many children to move their dolls about in a game they called Eviction.

"The Depression had pups on our doorstep." So said an Oklahoma farmer whose ill fortune had multiplied, although he was lucky enough to keep his doorstep. But the luckless were legion, homeless, and on the move. Foreclosed farmers became migratory field hands in the West. Sharecroppers drifted north, plodding from city to city in search of a job and a bread line. Ragged bands of youths roamed the country aimlessly, sleeping in hobo jungles. Naturally, all these wanderers suffered poignantly from cold, hunger, and disease. Not so naturally, many were denied relief because they had no legal residence.

Even those fortunate Americans who managed to live out the decade in well-heeled comfort were often shaken by the misery they saw or read about. One had to wince at the courage of an Arkansas family that walked 900 miles to apply for work; and then wince again at the bitter humor of a penniless southerner who announced, "When you gits down to your last bean, your backbone and your navel shakes dice to see which gits it."

By 1939 the worst was over; the Depression had made a hero of every sufferer who managed to survive. The names of the poor were largely lost to posterity. But the experience that scourged them survived, recorded with heartbreaking fidelity by photographers, reporters, and social workers. The words and pictures gathered by these chroniclers did more than capture the raw emotions of the moment. They captured the soul of the Depression.

The Face
of Poverty

"Before daylight we were on the way to Chevrolet. The police were already on the job, waving us away from the office. 'Nothin' doin'. Nothin' doin'.' Now we were tramping through falling snow. Dodge employment office. A big well-fed man in a heavy overcoat stood at the door saying, 'No, no,' as we passed before him. On the tramp again. . . ."
—An unemployed autoworker

Desperate for work, a Detroiter advertises (right). Others bought jobs; one man paid a $10 fee to earn $13.50.

Jobless New Yorkers haunt the employment agencies on Sixth Avenue (opposite). One agency averaged 5,000 applicants a day—and had work for only 300.

A toil-worn California field hand faces an uncertain future. "I have worked hard all my life," said one man, "and all I have now is my broken body."

Ragged but tough, a South Carolina farm girl remains unintimidated. Many such children worked in the fields from "can see" to "can't see."

The Hand of Nature

"Oh, I tell you I've seen that old river come up. When it begins to git in the houses, we take and move everything up on the bank across the railroad tracks. Well, city folks come trotting up there with soup kettles. They's always one saying to another, 'Do you suppose them people's got little enough sense to go back to them shacks when the river goes down?' Yes Lord, we'll always go back to Shanty Town till the river rises some day and forgits to go down."
—A Tennessee squatter

The receding floodwater leaves mud and wreckage inside an Indiana farmhouse.

Adding to the burden of the Depression, the Ohio River invades Louisville in 1937. In that year of high water, a million people needed flood relief.

Flood victims line up for food and pure water. Said a relief worker, "It ain't going to hurt the government to feed and clothe them that needs it."

"When these winds hit us, we and our misery were suddenly covered with dust. Here in the Texas Panhandle we were hit harder than most anywhere else. If the wind blew one way, here came the dark dust from Oklahoma. Another way and it was the gray dust from Kansas. Still another way, the brown dust from Colorado and New Mexico. Little farms were buried. And the towns were blackened."
—A Texas farmer

"These storms were like rolling black smoke. We had to keep the lights on all day. We went to school with headlights on, and with dust masks on. I saw a woman who thought the world was coming to an end. She dropped down on her knees in the middle of Main Street in Amarillo and prayed out loud, 'Dear Lord! Please give them another chance.'"
—A Texas schoolboy

After years of drought, the great dust storm of May 21, 1937, strikes Clayton, New Mexico. Despite dust masks, many died of suffocation.

"All that dust made some of the farmers leave; they became the Okies. We stuck it out here. We scratched, literally scratched, to live. We'd come to town to sell sour cream for nine cents a pound. If we could find a town big enough and far enough away from the dust, we could sell eggs at ten cents a dozen. Despite all the dust and the wind, we were putting in crops, but making no crops and barely living out of barnyard products only. We made five crop failures in five years."
—An Oklahoma farmer

"For Sale" signs such as this one marked the start of the dust bowlers' migrations.

An abandoned farm lies inundated by dust (right). Departing farmers reduced the population of Hall County, Texas, from 14,392 to only 7,000.

The Promise of the Road

Heading west, migrants gaze wearily from their car (right). For them, California, the "Land of Milk and Honey," would offer only drudgery and privation.

"This is a hard life to swallow, but I just couldn't sit back there and look to someone to feed us."
—A migratory worker

A nomad (below) looks across the desert: "Yessir, we're starved, stalled and stranded."

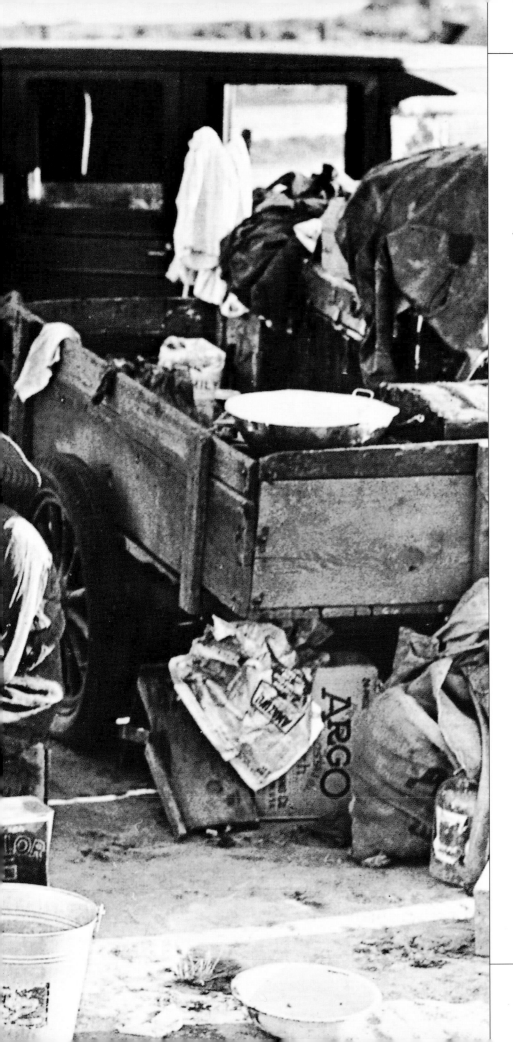

"October-December 1932. Cut Malaga and muscat grapes near Fresno. About $40 a month. December 1932. Left for Imperial Valley, Calif. February 1933. Picked peas, Imperial Valley. Earned $30 for season. On account of weather, was fortunate to break even. March-April 1933. Left for Chicago. Returned to California. May 1933. Odd jobs on lawns and radios at Fresno. June 1933. Picked figs near Fresno. Earned $50 in two months."
—A migratory worker's logbook

Rude cardboard shacks served as winter quarters for migrants in California's Imperial Valley.

A large family, intact despite its migrations, gathers to share a simple meal. "Us people has got to stick together to get by these hard times."

A Tennessee woman (left) succumbs to despondency: "I've wrote back that we're well and such as that, but I never have wrote that we live in a tent."

A worker improvises his morning shave (below). In some camps shaving was a luxury: "You can't waste water when it costs so much to get."

"When they need us they call us migrants. When we've picked their crops we're bums and we've got to get out."
—A migratory worker

"We make as much as is fitten for such as us runnin'-around folks. Caint send the children to school we aint got the clothes. By a'savin up we get so's we can move on to the next place. We haven't had no help no way."
—A Texas migrant in California

Successful in California, a migrant woman admires her farm. Said she proudly, "One more piece of pipe and our water tank will be finished."

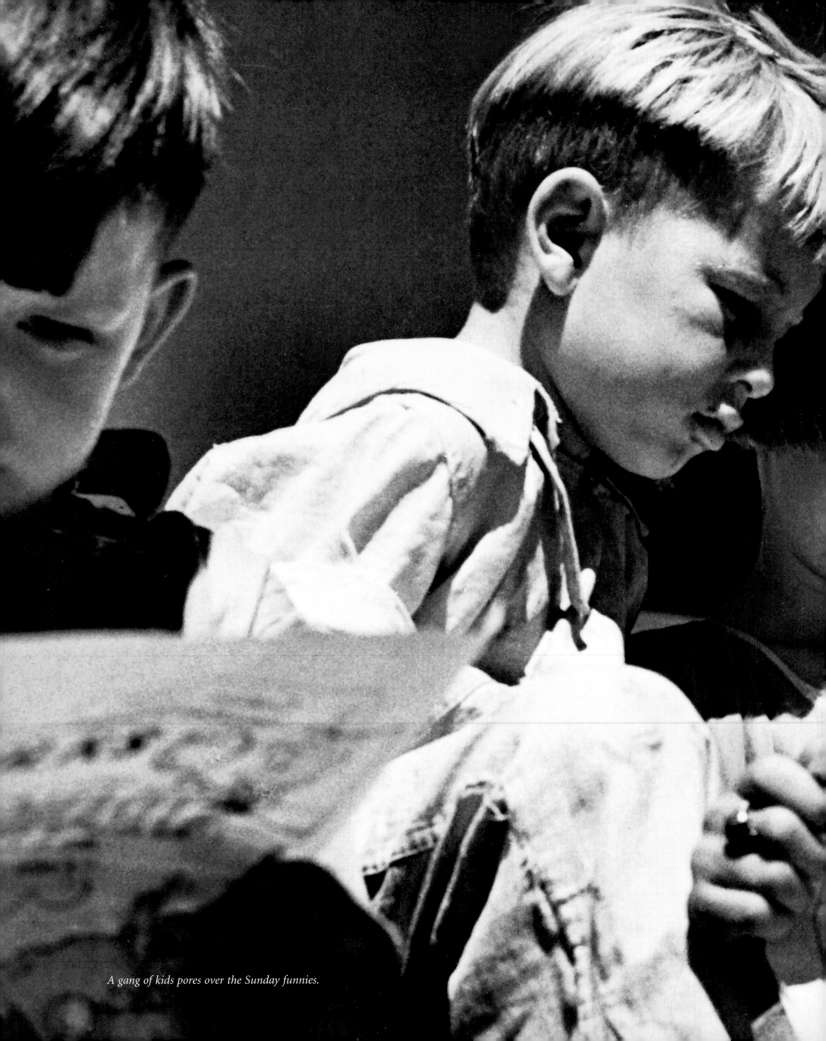

A gang of kids pores over the Sunday funnies.

Dream Factory

★

CHILDREN'S HEROES AND HEROINES

The Company of Heroes

During the '30s, the world of little kids orbited around a set of heroes and heroines whose extravagant lives were chronicled in a rich new range of media. Every Sunday before church, kids all over the country pawed through the funny papers for the latest exploits of Flash Gordon or Little Orphan Annie, whose pet expression "Leapin' Lizards!" was an American standard and whose faith in good old capitalism comforted many a Depression-ridden parent. On weekdays Annie also came booming over the radio, joined by the likes of hard-bitten detective Dick Tracy and Jack Armstrong, a teenage football hero. Saturday was movie day: four and a half raucous hours of cliffhanging serials featuring Tarzan or Flash Gordon, animated cartoons, and then perhaps a full-length picture starring that all-time heroine, Shirley Temple. In between times, the kids caught up on back adventures of the same characters through Big Little Books—squat, 400-page cubes of type and pictures that sold for a dime—or amused themselves with pop-up and cut-out books of Shirley, Buck Rogers, or a pair of overseas idols, Princesses Elizabeth and Margaret Rose of England.

The kingdoms of these heroes and heroines were even more varied than the media that brought them home to the kids; they ranged from America's playing fields to Oriental jungles, from the plains of the Old West to the slums of gangster-ridden cities, from Buckingham Palace to galaxies in the far reaches of outer space. And the idols themselves were just as varied in their makeup; some were real (the Little Princesses), some wholly fabricated (Buck Rogers), others physically real but fictitious in their exploits (Tom Mix and Shirley Temple).

The common ground on which these heroes and heroines stood was virtue, a commodity they sold in heaping portions by proving that clean living held unlimited rewards. With the exception of the Little Princesses, the idols also proved adept at selling commercial products. With each installment of their adventures, they fired off a barrage of sales pitches in behalf of various trinkets, toys, and breakfast foods. Little Orphan Annie even managed to pitch a drink called Ovaltine with her left hand while handing out her conservative, probusiness dogma with the right. Despite such blatant salesmanship, however, the most successful product served up was an inexpensive and wonderful world of make-believe, during times when the real world often seemed to be no fun at all.

Moppets, carefully coiffed and rehearsed by would-be movie mothers, participate in a Shirley Temple look-alike contest in Herrin, Illinois (opposite).

Little Orphan Annie

When Little Orphan Annie first appeared, she seemed out of place on the funny pages, for the simple reason that she was rarely funny. Rather, cartoonist Harold Gray time and again rallied his never-aging red-haired tyke and her mongrel Sandy to the aid of decent folks who were cowering before treacherous foreigners, mortgage holders, and crime lords. Often Annie's wealthy foster father, Oliver "Daddy" Warbucks, would happen by with his homicidal henchmen Punjab and the Asp to give Annie a hand.

Launched in 1924, the strip's success soon affected Annie's story line. Gray, who by 1934 was earning about $100,000 a year, began to color the melodrama with his conservative views on labor leaders and liberal politicians. Only when Annie went on radio did Gray compromise his—and the orphan's—philosophy of "ya hafta earn what ya get"; Annie gave away a glittering array of premiums in exchange for seals from the jars of sponsor Ovaltine's chocolate-milk mix. However, $1,000 a week soothed Gray's anguish at the thought of all those free rings, badges, shake-up mugs, and those secret-code cards *(right)* that allowed Annie's radio followers to decode such momentous messages as 8-36-18-28-22/30-44-2-24-40-18-28-10.

Annie rings

Buttons

Shake-up mug

Radio Orphan Annie's Secret Society

WARNING! Take good care of this book! It is the official Rulebook containing the secrets that only a member of Radio Orphan Annie's Secret Society may know. These secrets are **strictly private**—only for the eyes of members, and their parents, who are considered as **honorary members** . . . If it should be accidentally lost, anyone who finds it should return it at once, **without reading**, to the owner whose name is on the back cover.

Radio Orphan Annie's Secret Code

HERE is a special mystery code that Annie has worked out for broadcasting secret messages over the radio—a code that no one who is not on the inside will be able to understand. And because it's going to be used a lot, you want to learn it right away.

And another thing—always have a pencil and paper with you every night when you listen to Little Orphan Annie. Because you never know when one of these secret messages is going to come over the air. And you always want to be ready to write them down.

And now here's the code itself . . . The idea is simply this: Numbers take the place of letters. And because only the **even** numbers are used, Annie sometimes calls it the "Even-Number Mystery Code." For example, the number "2" stands for the letter "A"; and the number "4" stands for the letter "B"; the letter "C", etc.

And this is the way you use the code to write the secret message you want to send: simply substitute the number . . .

See how easy it is . . . Practice it every day . . .

IMPORTANT: Below is a handy chart, showing just how the Mystery Code works. Always take it to the radio when you listen to Little Orphan Annie. And if you ever mislay your chart and can't find it, remember that it's called the **EVEN-NUMBER** Code, so that you can easily make another one on a piece of paper to use in case anything ever happens to this.

2 A	4 B	6 C	8 D	10 E	12 F
14 G	16 H	18 I	20 J	22 K	24 L
26 M	28 N	30 O	32 P	34 Q	36 R
38 S	40 T	42 U	44 V	46 W	48 X
50 Y	52 Z	54 &			

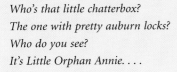

Secret society badges and code

Bracelets

Little Orphan Annie's Song

Who's that little chatterbox?
The one with pretty auburn locks?
Who do you see?
It's Little Orphan Annie. . . .

Bright eyes, cheeks a rosy glow,
There's a store of healthiness handy.
Mite-size, always on the go.
And if you want to know—"Arf!" says Sandy. . . .

Flash Gordon

When the planet Mongo threatened to collide with Earth in 1934, Yale-bred polo player Flash Gordon and a beautiful girl named Dale Arden were kidnapped aboard the rocket of crazed genius Hans Zarkov. With that notion for openers, cartoonist Alex Raymond launched the Flash Gordon story, first on the comic pages and eventually on the screen and in Big Little Books.

Guided by Raymond's fertile imagination, Flash, Dale, and Dr. Zarkov journeyed from Earth to Mongo; during the trip Zarkov miraculously regained his sanity, having first calculated that the runaway planet would miss Earth. Though the folks at home were now presumably safe, Flash and his friends were not, for Mongo was ruled by yellow-skinned, almond-eyed Ming the Merciless, who was evil incarnate in the '30s, when Americans were fretting increasingly over the Yellow Peril of emerging Asia. On Mongo, Flash was ever the target of sensual women and unspeakably foul agents of the wily Ming. Yet he remained true both to Dale and to the values of the Yale polo field (as interpreted by Raymond): "This was a Tournament of Death, but it was still to be fought by heroes imbued with the ideals of sportsmanship and fair play."

In films, Olympic swim star Buster Crabbe played a peroxided Flash.

Pedometer

Hovering discs and gun

Jack Armstrong

The All-American Boy!!" As the radio announcer shouted those magic words and a male chorus swung into the "Hudson High Fight Song," millions of kids began to live through the latest adventure of brainy, brawny, awesomely pure-in-heart Jack Armstrong. The All-American Boy's missions were three: to lead Hudson High to athletic glory, to overcome all bad guys, and to peddle Wheaties. Naturally Jack broke all scoring records for Hudson High and for Wheaties, in whose behalf he unloaded tons of crispy wheat flakes and scads of premiums. At the same time the show served up heaping portions of fair play and love for America, the latter being shoehorned into every possible line of script—as witness the dialogue below.

Tell the boys and girls of the United States this world is theirs. If they have hearts of gold, a glorious new golden age awaits us. If they are honest, riches shall be theirs. If they are kind, they shall save the whole world from malice and meanness. Will you take that message to the boys and girls of the United States, Jack Armstrong?
—Tibetan monk to Jack Armstrong, 1939

The Wheaties Song

Won't you try Wheaties?
They're whole wheat with all of the bran.
Won't you try Wheaties?
For wheat is the best food of man.

Hudson High Fight Song

Wave the flag for Hudson High, boys,
Show them how we stand!
Ever shall our team be champions,
Known throughout the land!
Rah Rah Boola Boola Boola Boola.

Talisman and pieces
for chart game

Whistle ring

JACK ARMSTRONG'S
SECRET WHISTLE CODE

JACK ARMSTRONG

UNCLE JIM

INSTRUCTIONS

One Whistle . . . . (Short)
Attention

Two Whistles . . . . (Short)
Be on guard for trouble

Three Whistles . . . . . . (One long, two short)
In danger, come at once

Four Whistles . . . . (Short)
We're being watched

Two Whistles . . . . (Two Long)
Important news —
meet me at once

BETTY

BILLY

Tarzan

In 1914 a middle-aged hack writer named Edgar Rice Burroughs, who had collected rejection slips from every major American publisher, finally sold his first novel, *Tarzan of the Apes.* This bizarre adventure story, set in the jungles of darkest Africa, told of the nurturing of an orphaned year-old boy, scion of the English House of Greystoke, by a fierce she-ape named Kala. In Kala's warm embrace, both Tarzan (which means "white skin" in ape language) and Edgar Rice Burroughs grew and prospered.

By the end of the '30s, Tarzan was the established hero of 21 fast-selling novels, a deftly drawn comic strip *(above),* a 15-minute daily radio serial, and 16 movies. Most popular with Tarzan fans in this decade were the movies, with their "take-me-to-the-elephant-graveyard" plots and their deathless dialogue, the best of it uttered by Olympic swim star Johnny Weissmuller during his incumbency in the title role.

In his first film, *Tarzan, the Ape Man (right),* Weissmuller enlarged the American vocabulary with the line "Me Tarzan, you Jane" and also introduced his fearful jungle yodel, a mixture of five sounds that included his own scream, a soprano singing high C, and a recording of a hyena's howl played backward.

1. In an early scene, ivory hunters James Parker and Harry Holt quiz natives about the elephant graveyard.

2. The safari, including Maureen O'Sullivan as Parker's daughter Jane, finds its path blocked by Tarzan.

3. Infatuated by Jane, Tarzan kidnaps her. At first, she balks at sharing Tarzan's tree house with either him or his chum Cheta.

4. Jane falls for Tarzan and teaches him to speak. During a lakeside frolic, he utters the immortal "Me Tarzan, you Jane."

5. Conscience-smitten, Jane returns to her father as the safari is captured by Pygmies; Tarzan and his pals swing to the rescue.

FADEOUT: The safari over, Jane becomes the mate of Tarzan, who takes her to the mountain for a view of her new domain.

Comic-book premium

Membership oath

Autographed photo of Tony and Tom

Membership song

Tom Mix

Reach for the sky! Lawbreakers always lose, Straight Shooters always win!! It pays to shoot straight!!!" Young radio listeners thrilled to hear cowboy character Tom Mix bark out this instructive battle cry. Naturally, when their hero commanded them to eat his sponsor Ralston's wheat cereal, they hastened to do so; and when Tom said that a few Ralston box tops would yield the treasures shown here, what real Straight Shooter could resist?

Tom's radio fans had plenty of company in their worship of the hard-jawed idol. Long before the radio show began in 1933, Mix had built up an international following that had rooted for him and the Wonder Horse Tony through some 180 feature films.

In real life, the old Straight Shooter was an old rake who ran through three wives and four million dollars. Nevertheless he guarded his public image as a nonsmoking teetotaler. "I want to keep my pictures in such a vein that parents will not object to letting their children see me on the screen," explained Tom solemnly. And all his fans believed him, remaining loyal literally to the end: When he died in 1940, the Tom Mix Club of Lisbon, Portugal, gave up going to movies for two weeks as a sign of mourning.

Slide-whistle ring

Signature ring

Compass and magnifier

Club badge

Siren ring

Magnet ring

Mirror ring

Club ring

Horseshoe-nail ring

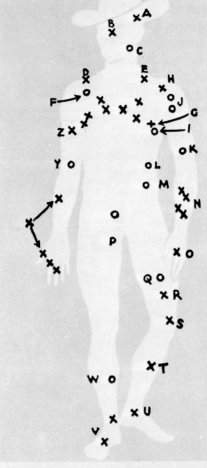

TOM MIX' INJURIES

Danger and difficulty have never daunted Tom Mix, nor broken bones stopped him. He has been blown up once, shot 12 times and injured 47 times in movie stunting. The chart shows the location of some of Tom's injuries. (X marks fractures; circles, bullet wounds.)

A. Skull fractured in accident.
B. Nose injured when artillery wagon blew up in China.
C. Shot thru jaw by sniper in Spanish-American War.
D. Shoulder fractured in circus accident.
E. Collar bone broken four times in falls.
F. Shot by bandit in Mix home.
G. Eight broken ribs from movie accidents.
H. Shoulder fractured when horse was shot from under him by bandits in U. S. Marshal days.
I. Shot by cattle rustlers in Texas.
J. Shot twice in left arm by Oklahoma outlaws.
K. Shot below elbow by outlaw.
L. Shot through abdomen by killer he arrested.
M. Wounded in gun fight with rustlers.
N. Left arm broken four times in movie stunting.
O. Hand broken in movie stunt.
P. Shot by bad man while Oklahoma sheriff.
Q. Shot in leg when 14 years old.
R. Leg trampled by horse.
S. Fractured knee in wagon accident.
T. Leg broken while stunting for movies.
U. Fractured ankle breaking wild horses.
V. Foot and ankle broken in wagon accident.
W. Shot through leg by bank robbers.
X. Three broken fingers, hand and arm fractured in screen fights and film stunting.
Y. Shot through elbow in real stage coach hold-up (1902).
Z. Broken arm in film stunting.

NOTE: Scars from twenty-two knife wounds are not indicated, nor is it possible to show on the diagram the hole four inches square and many inches deep that was blown in Tom's back by a dynamite explosion.

Wrangler badge

Decoder badge

Cowboy spur

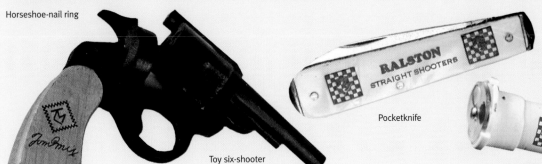

Toy six-shooter

Pocketknife

Flashlight

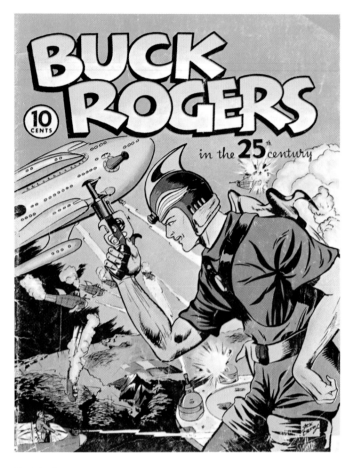

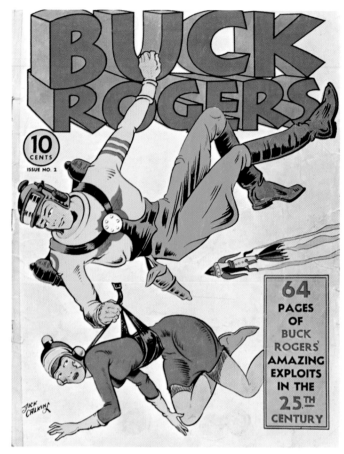

Comic books

Buck Rogers

Wilma, does all your equipment check out?" "Yes, Buck, I have my Thermic Radiation Projector, the Electrocosmic Spectrometer and the Super Radiating Protonoformer all set to go!" And so Buck Rogers and his luscious copilot Wilma Deering blasted off through the comics and radio on another mission to save "the whole universe."

All of Buck's adventures were marked by this same wild conglomeration of technological prophecy and sheer drivel, and the climax of each plot was woefully predictable: Buck would capture archvillains Killer Kane and the slinky Ardala and commit them to the intergalactic Rehabilitation Center—from which they somehow always managed to escape.

Killer and Ardala should have stayed put, for they were up against the combined brains and muscle of the Solar Scouts plus an ingenious arsenal of cosmic weapons that included rocket pistols, whose discharge introduced to the language the death sound ZAP, and atomic bombs. These weapons of the future were fascinating to Buck's 20th-century fans; when Macy's department store in New York advertised it had toy versions of Buck Rogers disintegrator guns, the next morning a queue of 20,000 people—a third of a mile long—awaited the store's opening.

Friction-powered rocket ships

Tootsie Toy rocket ships

Pop-up books

ATTACKED BY THE GIANT REPTILE

Water pistol

Disintegrator guns and holster

Rocket pistol

Detective badge

Rookie badge

Sophomore badge

Secret Service Patrol officer badges

Club button

Official watch

Dick Tracy

Dick Tracy, the sharp-profiled comic-strip detective, was a natural product of the '30s. Describing his cartoon creation, artist Chester Gould said, "Big gangsters were running wild but going to court and getting off scot free. I thought: why not have a guy who doesn't take the gangsters to court but shoots 'em?" So saying, Gould launched a strip loaded with gunfire. In the very first week, the slaying of Jeremiah Trueheart (right) marked the first time anyone had been gunned to death on the funny pages. More, much more, was to follow, for Dick Tracy, fiancé of Trueheart's

daughter Tess, was so moved by this foul deed that he signed on for life with the police force.

Quaker Oats cereal brought the detective to radio and soon devised a diabolically cunning sales gimmick: the Dick Tracy Secret Service Patrol. A boy's rise up the patrol hierarchy was directly proportional to how much Quaker Oats he could cram down, for a sergeant's badge cost five box tops, a lieutenant's seven, and so on. The company mercifully stopped the escalation at 15 box tops, but added a fillip for cereal-swelled candidates bucking for the ultimate rank of Inspector-General: They had to come up with a new Quaker Oats-gobbling recruit for the patrol.

Panels selected from the first two weeks of strips show how Dick Tracy's jaw began to jut dangerously after thugs slew his fiancée's father.

Elizabeth

Margaret Rose

The Little Princesses

On the morning of May 12, 1937, two pretty, curly-haired little girls in purple robes and golden coronets stood on a balcony alongside their parents and waved at a cheering throng. On that day Elizabeth and Margaret Rose Windsor of Great Britain *(above)* fulfilled a dream cherished by just about every little girl in the Western world: their daddy was crowned king—of England, no less—and they were going to live in a real palace.

Eleven-year-old Princess Elizabeth and six-year-old Princess Margaret Rose quickly became international heroines and the subjects of a batch of hastily assembled biographies, storybooks (including one told from the viewpoint of their pet dogs), and paper-doll books. With the latter, a little girl anywhere could cut out dresses, fold the tabs over punch-out figures *(left),* and together with her own two princess pals, dream through a delicious range of royal fantasies, including a private coronation.

Shirley Temple

My first impression of Shirley was a bit of sunshine. She had on a yellow dress and yellow coat and all that golden hair." This loving commentary by Shirley Temple's studio schoolteacher summed up the doting affection of the whole nation for the blonde moppet who swiftly became the child of the decade after she sang and danced, at the age of five, in the 1934 movie *Stand Up and Cheer.*

In one of the many films that followed, Shirley was "Little Miss Marker"; she might well have been called "Little Miss Mark-Up" in real life. As Hollywood's top box-office draw from 1935 to 1938, her average of four

pictures a year grossed five million dollars annually and was credited with keeping her studio solvent.

Miss Temple's yearly $300,000 salary was boosted by royalties from a swarm of merchandisers of Shirley-endorsed dolls, doll clothes and accessories, soap, books, and ribbons. Her doll manufacturer alone sold some six million toy moppets—at $3 to $30 each—in boxes bearing the star's own childish scrawl. Outfits for these dolls often cost more than dresses for real girls. Even hairdressers profited from the star's popularity; they were besieged by girls demanding golden, labor-intensive 56-curled hairdos, just like Shirley's.

Cops and Robbers

★

The wages of crime for Bonnie and Clyde is death in this bullet-ridden auto.

The Daredevil Crooks

Hard times brought a marked boom for at least one profession—crime. While legitimate businesses closed and farms lay barren, an alarming number of Americans began looking for easy money through robbery, kidnapping, and even murder. Across the Midwest, bands of marauders traveling in fast-moving cars and toting sawed-off shotguns and Tommy guns began knocking over rural banks and post offices. In large cities, tightly organized undergrounds were raking in millions of dollars through extortion, prostitution, and auto-theft rings. By 1935, according to one estimate by the Justice Department, so many Americans had moved to the shady side of the law that crooks outnumbered carpenters by four to one, grocers by six to one, and doctors by 20 to one.

The first of the lawbreakers to win real notoriety, and surely the most hated criminal of his time, was an ex-convict from Germany named Bruno Richard Hauptmann. On the night of March 1, 1932, he climbed up to a second-story nursery bedroom in Hopewell, New Jersey, and kidnapped the 20-month-old son of aviation hero Charles Lindbergh. The nation was stunned. It was as though Hauptmann had violated every home in America. For Lindy was the country's favorite hero, a modest, tousle-haired symbol of American courage and integrity. Though Lindy paid $50,000 in ransom, the baby was found dead six weeks later. When Hauptmann was finally caught and executed in the electric chair, the country registered deep satisfaction.

But the country had some strikingly different feelings about other crimes and criminals; many people, impoverished and embittered by the Depression, actually found a certain justice in the mounting number of bank robberies. The most notorious of the bank thieves, John Dillinger *(opposite),* even emerged as a kind of Robin Hood folk hero. "Dillinger did not rob poor people. He robbed those who became rich by robbing the poor," wrote an admirer in Indianapolis. "I am for Johnnie." Indeed, Dillinger projected an image of swashbuckling glamour and generosity. Once, when he broke out with two hostages from a supposedly escape-proof Indiana jail, he gave the men four dollars carfare home. In their admiration, Dillinger's fans managed to forget that their hero had gunned down 10 men during his career, and that—like the other bandits shown on the following pages—he was basically just a cold-blooded thug.

"Johnnie's just an ordinary fellow. Of course, he goes out and holds up banks and things, but he's really just like any other fellow, aside from that."

A friend of John Dillinger

America's no. 1 desperado, John Dillinger (opposite), smiles as he shows off some of the tools of his trade: a Thompson submachine gun and a pistol.

GET·DILLINGER!

$15,000 *Reward*

═══ A PROCLAMATION ═══

WHEREAS, One John Dillinger stands charged officially with numerous felonies including murder in several states and his banditry and depredation stamp him as an outlaw, a fugitive from justice and a vicious menace to life and property;

NOW, THEREFORE, We, Paul McNutt, Governor of Indiana; George White, Governor of Ohio; F. B. Olson, Governor of Minnesota; William A. Comstock, Governor of Michigan; and Henry Horner, Governor of Illinois, do hereby proclaim and offer a reward of Five Thousand Dollars ($5,000.00) to, be paid to the person or persons who apprehend and deliver the said John Dillinger into the custody of any sheriff of any of the above-mentioned states or his duly authorized agent.

THIS IS IN ADDITION TO THE $10,000.00 OFFERED BY THE FEDERAL GOVERNMENT FOR THE ARREST OF JOHN DILLINGER.

HERE IS HIS FINGERPRINT CLASSIFICATION and DESCRIPTION. ——— FILE THIS FOR IDENTIFICATION PURPOSES.

John Dillinger. (w) age 30 yrs., 5-8½, 180½ lbs., gray eyes. med. chest. hair, med. comp.. med. build. Dayton. O.. P. D. No. 10587. O. S. E. No. 559-646.

F.P.C. (12)

	M	9	R	O	O
	S	14	U	OO	8
13	10	O	O	O	
u	R	w	w	w	
5	11	15	I	8	
u	U	u	w	u	

FRONT VIEW

Be on the lookout for this desperado. He is heavily armed and usually is protected w i t h bullet - proof vest. Take no unnecessary chances in getting this man. He is thoroughly prepared to shoot his way out of any situation.

GET HIM

DEAD

OR ALIVE

Notify any Sheriff or Chief of Police of Indiana, Ohio, Minnesota, Michigan, Illinois.

or **THIS BUREAU**

SIDE VIEW

ILLINOIS STATE BUREAU OF CRIMINAL IDENTIFICATION AND INVESTIGATION

T. P. Sullivan, Supt.   Springfield, Illinois

Wanted for murder, robbery, and half a dozen other felonies, Dillinger grew a moustache and altered his fingerprints with acid to escape detection.

WANTED

LESTER M. GILLIS,

aliases GEORGE NELSON, "BABY FACE" NELSON, ALEX GILLIS, LESTER GILES,

"BIG GEORGE" NELSON, "JIMMIE", "JIMMY" WILLIAMS .

On June 23, 1934, HOMER S. CUMMINGS, Attorney General of the United States, under the authority vested in him by an Act of Congress approved June 6, 1934, offered a reward of

$5,000.00

for the capture of Lester M. Gillis or a reward of

$2,500.00

for information leading to the arrest of Lester M. Gillis.

DESCRIPTION

Age, 25 years; Height, 5 feet 4-3/4 inches; Weight, 133 pounds; Build, medium; Eyes, yellow and grey slate; Hair, light chestnut; Complexion, light; Occupation, oiler.

All claims to any of the aforesaid rewards and all questions and disputes that may arise as among claimants to the foregoing rewards shall be passed upon by the Attorney General and his decisions shall be final and conclusive. The right is reserved to divide and allocate portions of any of said rewards as between several claimants. No part of the aforesaid rewards shall be paid to any official or employee of the Department of Justice.

If you are in possession of any information concerning the whereabouts of Lester M. Gillis communicate immediately by telephone or telegraph collect to the nearest office of the Division of Investigation, United States Department of Justice, the local offices of which are se forth on the reverse side of this notice.

The apprehension of Lester M. Gillis is sought in connection with the murder of Special Agent W. C. Baum of the Division of Investigation near Rhinelander, Wisconsin on April 23, 1934.

JOHN EDGAR HOOVER, DIRECTOR,
DIVISION OF INVESTIGATION,
UNITED STATES DEPARTMENT OF JUSTICE,
WASHINGTON, D. C.

June 25, 1934

Pint-sized Baby Face Nelson, a gunslinger for Dillinger, was sought in 10 states by 5,000 police, 300 infantrymen, the FBI, and several airplanes.

Machine Gun Kelly and His Mrs.

George Kelly

Kate Kelly

George Kelly, who was so hot with a Tommy gun that he could write his name with bullets on a barn door, started out as a small-time bootlegger. He probably would have stayed small had it not been for the ambition of his wife, Kathryn, an ex-manicurist. Kate pressured her husband into moving up to high-powered capers like bank robbery, kidnapping, and murder, and enhanced his prestige among fellow crooks by passing out empty shell casings from his machine gun as souvenirs.

George and Kate Kelly, shown both in the mug shots above and in a cuddly snapshot, were a notorious husband-and-wife team.

Pretty Boy Floyd

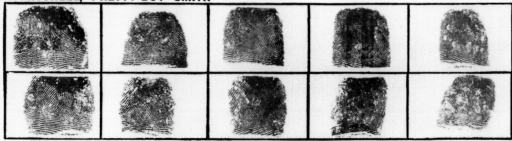

DESCRIPTION

Age, 26 years
Height, 5 feet, 8¼ inches
Weight, 155 pounds
Hair, dark
Eyes, gray
Complexion, medium
Nationality, American
Scars and marks, 1 Vac. cic.
1 tattoo (Nurse in Rose)

CRIMINAL RECORD

As Charles Arthur Floyd, No. 22318, arrested police department, St. Louis, Missouri, September 16, 1925; charge, highway robbery.
As Charles Floyd, No. 29078, received S.P., Jefferson City, Missouri, December 18, 1925, from St. Louis; crime, robbery, first degree; sentence, 5 years.
As Charles A. Floyd, No. 16950, arrested police department,

Kansas City, Missouri, March 9, 1929; charge, investigation.
As Charles Floyd, No. 3999, arrested police department, Kansas City, Kansas, May 6, 1929; charge, vagrancy and suspicion - highway robbery; released May 7, 1929.
As Charles Floyd, No. 887, arrested police department, Pueblo, Colorado, May 9, 1929; charge, vagrancy; fined $50 and sentenced to serve 60 days in jail.
As Frank Mitchell, No. 19983, arrested police department, Akron, Ohio, March 8, 1930; charge, investigation.
As Charles Arthur Floyd, No. 21458, arrested police department, Toledo, Ohio, May 20, 1930; charge, suspicion.
As Charles Arthur Floyd, sentenced November 24, 1930, to serve from 12 to 15 years in Ohio State Penitentiary (bank robbery, Sylvania, Ohio); escaped enroute to penitentiary.

Charles Arthur Floyd is wanted in connection with the murder of Otto Reed, Chief of Police of McAlester, Oklahoma, William J. Grooms and Frank E. Hermanson, police officers of Kansas City, Missouri, Raymond J. Caffrey, Special Agent of the United States Bureau of Investigation, and their prisoner, Frank Nash, at Kansas City, Missouri, on June 17, 1933.
Law enforcement agencies kindly transmit any additional information or criminal record to nearest office, United States Bureau of Investigation.
If apprehended, please notify Special Agent in Charge, United States Bureau of Investigation, 905 Federal Reserve Bank Building, Kansas City, Missouri, and the Director, United States Bureau of Investigation, Department of Justice, Washington, D. C.

(over)   Issued by: J. Edgar Hoover, Director

Gray eyed and wavy haired, Floyd was hunted by the FBI for gunning down four lawmen in Kansas City in 1933.

An enfant terrible of the underworld, Charles "Pretty Boy" Floyd took up crime at age 18 by robbing a local post office of $350 in pennies. During the next 12 years he was reputed to have robbed more than 30 midwestern banks; in 1932 his score in Oklahoma alone was so high that the state's bank-insurance rates doubled. Floyd was equally adept at shooting people. The latter talent gave him such satisfaction that he filed 10 notches in his pocket watch to remind him of the number of men he had killed.

Ma Barker and Her Boys

Dock Barker

Freddie Barker

Arizona Clark "Ma" Barker, who believed in crime for the whole family, reared her four sons to be God-fearing, obedient thugs. Each Sunday she dragged them off to church; weekdays she schooled them in the finer points of thievery, kidnapping, and murder. The Barkers shown here, joined by brothers Herman and Lloyd—and occasionally by other gangland luminaries—pulled off so many audacious capers that they became the all-time leaders in major crime, family style.

Key members of the Barker gang included Dock and Freddie (above), and Ma, shown at right with boyfriend Arthur Dunlop.

Bonnie and Clyde

WANTED FOR MURDER
JOPLIN, MISSOURI

F.P.C.29 - MO. 9
26 U 00 6

CLYDE CHAMPION BARROW, age 24, 5'7",130#,hair dark brown and
wavy,eyes hazel,light complexion,home West Dallas,Texas.
This man killed Detective Harry McGinnis and Constable
J.W. Harryman in this city,April 13, 1933.

BONNIE PARKER   CLYDE BARROW   CLYDE BARROW

This man is dangerous and is known to have committed the following
murders: Howard Hall, Sherman, Texas; J.N.Bucher,Hillsboro, Texas;
a deputy sheriff at Atoka, Okla; deputy sheriff at West Dallas,
Texas; also a man at Belden, Texas.
        The above photos are kodaks taken by Barrow and his com-
panions in various poses,and we believe they are better for
identification than regular police pictures.
        Wire or write any information to the

                        Police Department.

The Barrow gang's fondness for hamming in front of a Kodak made identification easier for pursuing lawmen.

The most sadistic of the decade's hoods, Clyde Barrow shot down people for the sheer love of killing. Barrow embarked on a murder-and-robbery spree through the states of Missouri, Texas, and Oklahoma with his moll, cigar-chomping Bonnie Parker, and a succession of young men. Ill tempered and somewhat effeminate, Barrow was generally despised by other midwestern bandits, who felt that his haphazard killings and frequently bungled robberies lowered the standards of the profession.

Clear eyed, attentive, all his energies focused on the task at hand, Director J. Edgar Hoover of the FBI pursues a hot lead over the telephone.

The Hero Cop

Following the Lindbergh kidnapping in 1932, a new race of hoodlums suddenly rose up, and alarming statistics appeared in the news: America had the highest homicide rate in the world; two banks were being robbed a day; crime was costing each American $140 a year. And the Justice Department claimed 400,000 hoods were on the loose.

Furthermore, state and local police couldn't cope with the epidemic. Often, while tracking down a gang, they would find that the quarry had slipped into the next state and hence out of their jurisdiction. Something radical needed to be done. Alarmists suggested that martial law be declared and the army called in. J. Edgar Hoover *(left)* had a better idea.

Eight years after becoming director of the Justice Department's Bureau of Investigation, he had transformed it from the attorney general's private gumshoe operation to an effective crime-fighting machine. He had instituted stringent hiring standards and codes of conduct, gathered a huge file of fingerprints, and set up a crime lab for examining evidence. The bureau was ready and able to tackle the job, he reported. All he needed was an okay from Congress, removing limitations on its tactics and enlarging the number of federal crimes on which it could act.

The "Lindbergh Law," which for all practical purposes made snatching a federal crime, thus allowing the G-men to chase kidnappers, was passed in mid-1932. Other new laws followed, making robberies of national banks, illegal use of telephone and telegraph wires, and virtually any other type of crime that crossed a state line fair game for the G-men. Agents were also authorized to make arrests and carry firearms.

Hoover's posse of crimebusters soon began running down desperadoes. They quickly nailed:

• John Dillinger, Public Enemy No. 1. A brothelkeeper betrayed him to the Feds. In July 1934, in front of a Chicago movie house, an attack force gunned him down.

• Baby Face Nelson, a particularly vicious pal of Dillinger's. Nelson was spotted in a Chicago suburb in November 1934 and was fatally wounded, but not before he took the lives of two federal agents.

• Charles "Pretty Boy" Floyd—shot to death while battling G-men on an Ohio farm in October 1934.

• Arizona Clark "Ma" Barker, who died with her son Freddie at her hideout in Oklawaha, Florida, in 1935.

• George "Machine Gun" Kelly, who gave the federal investigators their nickname. In 1933 agents crashed into his hideout. He yelled, "Don't shoot, G-men, don't shoot!" He said "G-men" was short for "Government men."

Other criminals fell to the G-men as well. As the tally mounted, Hoover and his agents became heroes. "The nation has waited with the patience of a Job for this hour," extolled the *St. Louis Post-Dispatch.* "In a determined Department of Justice backed by the resources of the national Government, gangsters face an invincible foe."

In 1935 (the year the word "federal" was added to the bureau's name) Hollywood got into the act. Warner Bros. premiered *G-Men,* in which James Cagney as the intrepid agent brought to justice the nation's worst public enemy and got the girl as well. Meanwhile, children began sporting tin G-man badges, toting toy Tommy guns, wearing G-man underwear, and sleeping in G-man pajamas. "Pick a small boy these days and ask him who of all the people in the world he wants to be like," wrote the New York *World-Telegram* in 1936, "and ten to one he will reply— J. Edgar Hoover."

Police who had once welcomed the Feds' assistance grumbled that the director was grabbing too much limelight while other critics voiced a more serious complaint—that the zealous Hoover might be encroaching on civil liberties. But most Americans admired him and shared his beliefs about the need for law and order. In their eyes, the line between the good guys and the bad guys was still fairly clear, and the job of the nation's top crime-fighter, as Hoover often said, was never done.

FDR

★

THE BOSS, THE DYNAMO

Undismayed by his critics, a relaxed FDR radiates confidence. "He must have been psychoanalyzed by God," declared an awed associate.

VANITY FAIR

FEBRUARY 1934
PRICE 35 CENTS

That Man in the White House

When Franklin D. Roosevelt became the 32nd president of the United States, the country was scared. That morning, March 4, 1933, every bank in the nation had had to close its doors. The old leaders were ashen faced. "I'm afraid," said the chairman of Bethlehem Steel, Charles Schwab, "every man is afraid."

On the high inaugural platform, in front of the Capitol, the 51-year-old president-elect repeated the oath of office in a clear, deliberate voice and said, "This Nation asks for action, and action now." Entering his car to go to the White House, he clasped his hands over his head in the salute of a champion. The next morning, rolling in a wheelchair as he had since he was disabled by polio 12 years before, Roosevelt moved into the Oval Office, sat alone for a few moments, then shouted for his aides and began to act, starting with a call for a special session of Congress. His emergency banking bill strengthening the financial system roared through the House unchanged in 38 minutes. When the banks reopened four days later, deposits exceeded withdrawals. The immediate panic was over. Confidence was beginning to return.

Sensing opportunity, FDR kept the lawmakers in session. In the next 100 days, riding herd on the nation with a firmer rein than it had felt since the days of his cousin, Teddy Roosevelt, he altered the conduct of American life. Fifteen major messages streamed from the White House to Capitol Hill. When Congress adjourned on June 16, 15 new laws assured government action: laws to employ the jobless, to develop the Tennessee Valley, to support crop prices, to repeal Prohibition, to stop home foreclosures, to insure bank deposits, to stabilize the economy, and more.

FDR called the program a "New Deal" for the nation, but others thought it went beyond that. "We have had our revolution," said *Collier's* magazine. "We like it." The people raised their heads; even the well-to-do were at first delighted. As Roosevelt had noted, action, any kind of action, had been their plea. Kansas's Republican governor, Alf Landon, had said, "Even the iron hand of a dictator is in preference to a paralytic stroke." Now industrialist Pierre du Pont sent FDR a friendly letter. And press lord William Randolph Hearst flattered FDR: "I guess at your next election we will make it unanimous."

> "Never was there such a change in the transfer of a government. The President is the boss, the dynamo, the works."

Arthur Krock in the *New York Times*, March 12, 1933

In 1934, Vanity Fair *recorded the people's pleasure in another self-assured Rough Rider named Roosevelt who could tame the country (opposite).*

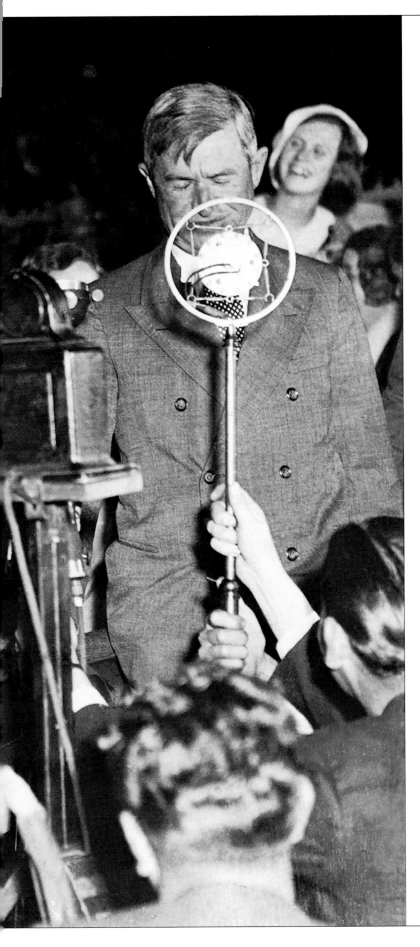

The Style of the New President

The new president surprised a lot of people. Before the election the best thinkers considered him a lightweight—"a pleasant man who, without any important qualifications, would very much like to be President," as pundit Walter Lippmann wrote. But the critics soon realized that FDR's easy quips and laughter reflected not vacuous amiability but buoyant confidence, that here was a tough-minded man with a quick grasp of what had to be done. Accordingly Lippmann, for one, ate crow: "The nation which had lost confidence in everything and everybody has regained confidence in the government and in itself."

"How do you account for him?" gasped Kansas editor William Allen White. "Was I just fooled before the election, or has he developed?" The quotation below from cowboy entertainer-philosopher Will Rogers expressed the nation's delight at the new man in the White House.

"I will say one thing for this Administration. It's the only time when the fellow with money is worrying more than the one without it."

October 3, 1933

FDR howls along with (from left to right) son James, William McAdoo, and adviser James Farley as Will Rogers gets off a sly introduction in 1932.

The Personal Touch

In the '30s George M. Cohan, star of the Broadway musical *I'd Rather Be Right*, used to break up the audience by saying, "Bring me another fireside, I'm going on the air." Everyone knew he was joshing Roosevelt's own personal bit of show biz—the Fireside Chats. These were informal radio talks FDR delivered to the nation as Americans were relaxing after dinner. It was his favorite way of selling his programs and, in the face of Establishment and press hostility, it was indispensable in winning support for the New Deal. When the president's calm, resonant voice intoned "My friends," most Americans felt they were.

Inevitably, the Fireside Chats invited spoofing, some of it nasty, some as gentle as Cohan's wisecrack and the 1935 *Esquire* cartoon at right, showing FDR's wife, Eleanor, looking on as he broadcasts while his grandchildren badger him to hurry and get off the air. But the Fireside Chats were deadly serious, both for FDR and for the country. The first one, explaining the bank crisis, was decisive in reversing the panic. Here, in part, is what people heard on their radios that evening of March 12, 1933.

"You must have faith; you must not be stampeded by rumors."

FDR, March 12, 1933

I want to tell you what has been done in the last few days, why it was done, and what the next steps are going to be. First of all, let me state the simple fact that when you deposit money in a bank the bank does not put the money into a safe deposit vault. It invests your money in many different forms of credit—bonds, mortgages. In other words, the bank puts your money to work to keep the wheels turning around. A comparatively small part of the money is kept in currency—sufficient to cover the cash needs of the average citizen. In other words, the total amount of all the currency in the country is only a small fraction of the total deposits in all of the banks. What, then, happened? Because of undermined confidence, there was a general rush to turn bank deposits into currency. On the spur of the moment it was, of course, impossible to sell perfectly sound assets of a bank and convert them into cash except at panic prices far below their real value.

It was then that I issued the proclamation for the nationwide bank holiday. The second step was the legislation passed by the Congress to extend the holiday and lift the ban of that holiday gradually. This law also gave authority to develop a program of rehabilitation of our banking facilities. The new law allows the twelve Federal Reserve Banks to issue additional currency backed by actual, good assets. As a result, we start tomorrow, Monday, opening banks in the twelve Federal Reserve Bank cities—banks which have already been found to be all right. On succeeding days banks in smaller places will resume business, subject, of course, to the Government's physical ability to make common sense checkups. When the banks resume a very few people who have not recovered from their fear may again begin withdrawals. Let me make clear that the banks will take care of all needs—and it is my belief that when the people find that they can get their money the phantom of fear will soon be laid. I assure you that it is safer to keep your money in a reopened bank than under the mattress.

There will be, of course, some banks unable to open without being reorganized. The new law allows the Government to assist in making these reorganizations quickly and effectively. I do not promise you that every bank will be reopened or that individual losses will not be suffered, but there will be no losses that possibly could have been avoided; and there would have been greater losses had we continued to drift. I can even promise you salvation for some at least of the sorely pressed banks. Confidence and courage are the essentials in our plan. You must have faith; you must not be stampeded by rumors. We have provided the machinery to restore our financial system; it is up to you to support and make it work. Together we cannot fail.

"Aw, gee, Gran'pop, you're runnin' over into Ed Wynn's program!"

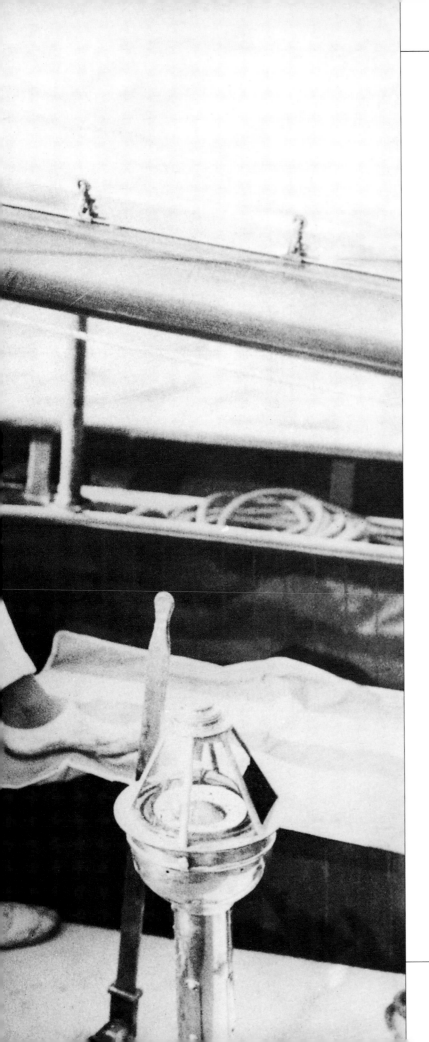

The Private Side

The second family of Roosevelts to move into the White House within a quarter century was an exciting batch of individualists with lots of verve and offspring. Each of FDR's children tended to go his or her own way, but Christmas Eve always found the clan gathered. Surrounded by grandchildren, FDR read from Dickens's *A Christmas Carol,* acting out the parts of Scrooge and Tiny Tim with gusto. Next day, at Christmas dinner, he carved paper-thin slices of turkey, boasting, "You can almost read through it."

As the presidency wore on, however, Roosevelt had less and less time for family matters. One day when a distraught son poured out his troubles, FDR absently handed him a paper, saying, "This is a most important document—I should like to have your opinion on it."

To restore his relationships with his children, and to restore himself after bearing the burdens of office, FDR turned to the sea, which he loved. Joyously he wrote back from a cruise, "The boys are having a grand time and we have one continuous kidding match." In 1934 he took Franklin Jr. and John on a 14,000-mile voyage aboard the cruiser *Houston.* They ranged from Haiti to Hawaii and FDR got another chance, denied him in Washington, to spend lazy hours with his boys. He reported home to his wife, who had long since given up sailing for horseback riding, "The boys are grand and really love it I think."

In an old sweater and flannels, FDR takes his son James sailing on the Amberjack II. Sailing, he told Secretary of the Interior Harold Ickes, was the only way he could really rest.

Eleanor

While FDR was revamping American political life, Eleanor Roosevelt broke the mold for presidential wives. Once a conventional society matron, she had spent 12 years being what her disabled husband called his eyes and ears, learning about politics and society's ills. She would be no genteel stay-at-home as first lady. Hardly had Eleanor moved into the White House before she began the unprecedented act of holding press conferences. What's more, she limited the invitation list to women reporters, forcing editors to hire newswomen if they wanted to get the story.

A mother of five and a grandmother as well, she ached for America's troubled youth, a quarter million of whom were homeless while millions more were hungry, ill clothed, and ill schooled. "I have moments of real terror," she said in 1934, "when I think we may be losing this generation." At her urging, FDR got Congress to create the National Youth Administration to help them with jobs and training.

Another cause—fair treatment for black Americans—put her far out in front of public opinion. Discovering that blacks in the South were being shut out of New Deal benefits, she persuaded FDR to ban the practice. She thumbed her nose at an Alabama Jim Crow law by perching between the white and Negro sections at a Birmingham meeting. She fought for antilynching legislation. And she quit the Daughters of the American Revolution after that outfit barred black singer Marian Anderson from its Constitution Hall in Washington.

Eleanor's activism earned the gratitude of millions as well as savage derision. FDR sometimes exploited her care for the downtrodden to gain their votes while keeping himself aloof to pacify more reactionary Democrats. But she often won him over to her causes, launching prodigies of persuasion with "Franklin, I think you should. . ." or "Franklin, surely you would not. . . ."

In 1936 she cast a wider net for her persuasive powers when she began writing a daily syndicated newspaper column called "My Day." She would use the forum to air her often controversial views for the rest of her life.

A warm moment reveals the couple's mutual affection. Both were energetic and strong willed. Eleanor believed FDR might have preferred a less critical wife.

Putting her convictions in public view, Eleanor poses for the press while calling on some black children.

For once less than earnest, the first lady cuts a rug.

The National Recovery Administration emblem appeared on any usable empty space.

The Alphabet Agencies: NRA and CCC

As FDR put his New Deal into effect, Congress spawned dozens of acts and agencies to carry the government's new burdens. Given long names, these organizations became known by their initials, which, added together, made up an entire alphabet of recovery measures. The office that excited the fiercest partisanship was the NRA (National Recovery Administration), created to regulate wages, working hours, and, indirectly, prices.

Most ordinary Americans greeted the NRA enthusiastically. Posters with the Blue Eagle symbol *(left)* were splashed everywhere, and big cities staged monster rallies to show support of the NRA codes. In New York, 250,000 people marched up Fifth Avenue to the music of 200 bands. In Tulsa, the hometown of NRA director Hugh Johnson, his 77-year-old mother led a parade and warned, "People had better obey the NRA because my son will enforce it like lightning, and you can never tell when lightning will strike." As columnist Heywood Broun prophesied, these parades had a lasting issue of new hope and confidence: "When a line forms and your shoulder touches that of a fellow and a comrade, solidarity is about to be born."

New Deal opponents kept up a barrage of criticism, of course. Businessmen damned the NRA as "creeping socialism." Union men called it "business fascism." And the Hearst newspapers suggested bitterly that what the initials NRA really stood for was "No Recovery Allowed." Yet not even the angriest opponents of the New Deal had much to say against the good works initiated by the CCC (Civilian Conservation Corps). In its nine years of existence, the CCC took some 2.5 million young men from the ranks of the unemployed, paid them $30 a month (most of it automatically sent to the home folks), and put them to work planting 200 million trees, fighting pine-twig blight and Dutch elm disease, digging drainage ditches and fishponds, building firebreaks and reservoirs, clearing beaches and camping grounds, and even restoring historic battlefields. This massive effort of conservation and reforestation benefited not only the nation but the boys themselves. One declared, "It made a man of me all right." Said another man, "If a boy wants to go and get a job after he's been in the C's, he'll know how to work."

CCC boys give three cheers at Camp Dix, New Jersey, after their first day. The average enlistee was a 20-year-old from a large family on relief.

PWA

To make jobs and stimulate business, Roosevelt in 1933 persuaded Congress to create the federally financed PWA (Public Works Administration)—and thereby changed the face of America. Armies of workmen for the PWA built a water-supply system for Denver; a flood-control system for Ohio's Muskingum Valley; a port for Brownsville, Texas; roads and bridges connecting Key West with the Florida mainland. A sampling of other PWA projects appears on these pages—but only a small sampling. Between 1933 and 1939 the PWA invested more than six billion dollars and 4.75 billion man-hours of labor in constructing about 10 percent of all the new transportation facilities built in the United States during the period, 35 percent of the new hospitals and health facilities, 65 percent of the city halls and courthouses and sewage disposal plants, and 70 percent of all educational buildings.

Because these projects were slow in developing, the president complemented the PWA with a nominally confusing addition to his alphabet soup, the WPA (Works Progress Administration). The main difference between the two agencies was that the PWA simply financed the projects, whereas the WPA handled the entire operation. In addition, the WPA found a new way to use its huge appropriations by making the federal government a big-time patron of the arts *(pages 114-115)*.

Municipal ferryboat, New York City

Electrification of Pennsylvania Railroad

Pavilion, Huntington Beach, California

Work shed, Grand Canyon National Park

Mental hospital, Camarillo, California

San Francisco Fair construction

Lincoln Tunnel, New York–New Jersey

Gold depository, Fort Knox, Kentucky

Triborough Bridge, New York City

Mall, Washington, D.C.

Prison farm, Tattnall County, Georgia

Boulder Dam, Colorado River

Zoo, Washington, D.C.

Swimming pool, Wheeling, West Virginia

Band shell, Phoenix, Arizona

Water tank, Sacramento, California

Floral conservatory, St. Louis

Federal Trade Commission, Washington, D.C.

WPA

Following the thesis that whenever possible a job-less man should be put in his own line of work, the WPA recruited thousands of unemployed artists and assigned them to projects paying up to $94.90 a month. Composers composed; musical anthropologists toured backwoods America recording folk songs; actors for the Federal Theatre entertained some 30 million people with shows. By decade's end, a whole generation of painters and writers had served its apprenticeship in the WPA. Admittedly, some artists were assigned work of questionable value. One writer made his bread and butter by taking a census of dogs in California's Monterey Peninsula. In 1939 the name of that writer and of his first major novel became household words: John Steinbeck and *The Grapes of Wrath.*

Actors sing in The Swing Mikado, *one of 1,200 WPA productions (above). At right, WPA artists are depicted at work by colleague Moses Soyer. Other WPA painters were Jackson Pollock, Willem de Kooning, and Ben Shahn.*

Labor

★

BLOOD BATTLES FOR WORKERS' RIGHTS

Cleveland cops move in as strikers overturn a foreman's car.

The Worker Finds a Voice

By the middle of the 1930s the American worker was stalking toward a deadly showdown with management. Thanks largely to the shrewd lobbying of bushy-browed John L. Lewis *(right)*, the formidable leader of the United Mine Workers (UMW), a federal law was on the books guaranteeing every laborer the right to join a union and use the union to bargain with his bosses. But acknowledging labor's rights by law was easier said than done. In many a big industrial town the only real law was the company's.

In those harsh times, firing was about the mildest punishment given a union organizer. A fair number of U.S. laborers actually worked at gunpoint. Why, a Senate committee had wanted to know in 1928, did the Pittsburgh Coal Company keep machine guns at its coal pits? "You cannot run the mines without them," replied Richard B. Mellon, chairman of the board. In 1935 hired guns still loomed over the toughest of the company towns, where a word for the union could get a man beaten up or killed.

When a strike was brewing in 1935 against the Akron, Ohio, tire manufacturers, the rubber companies had an army of strikebreakers standing by under the direction of one Pearl Bergoff, a king among strikebreakers. Pearl's delicate name mocked his nature. (His mother gave him the name she had picked for the daughter she wanted to have.) He ran a multimillion-dollar business, serving various major firms across the country, from an office in New York. His aides daily scanned out-of-town newspapers for hints of brewing strikes, whereupon Pearl dispatched one of his salesmen to peddle the Bergoff services. The deal included shipping a small army of men to fill the struck jobs and fitting them out with weapons from Pearl's armory of machine guns, night sticks, and tear gas.

Bergoff was not the only big-time goon for hire. The Pinkerton National Detective Agency, a favorite of the auto companies, earned $1,750,000 for its services to industry between 1933 and 1936. "We must do it," explained Vice President Herman L. Weckler of the Chrysler Corporation, "to obtain the information we need in dealing with our employees." By the mid '30s, however, industrial employees all over the country had long since become fed up with such dealing. And they were

> "Labor, like Israel, has many sorrows. Its women keep their fallen and they lament for the future of the children of the race."
>
> John L. Lewis

In 1936, labor czar John L. Lewis (opposite) blasts Republican presidential candidate Alf Landon as a "pitiful puppet responsible to the steel industry."

rallying behind Lewis, whose tough leadership and political power had brought a new era into view.

They could hardly have had a better man. Lewis had been in the thick of union wars for 25 years. As a teenager with a seventh-grade education, he had gone to work in the coal pits of Iowa with his five kid brothers. His awesome energies, angry convictions, and eloquent tongue soon won him a niche of his own in the United Mine Workers. A six-foot-three-inch bull of a man, Lewis had a mind as powerful as his imposing physique. At night and on union-organizing trips across the country, he read in their entirety the Bible, the *Odyssey* and the *Iliad*, Oswald Spengler and Shakespeare, Karl Marx and Friedrich Engels. By early 1934 this unique mixture of coal

"So I'm a Red? I suppose it makes me a Red because I don't like making time so hard on these goddamned machines. When I get home I'm so tired I can't sleep with my wife."

Assembly-line worker, 1935

miner, labor organizer, and reader of classics was entrenched as president of the UMW, and with the backing of the new federal law, he had built the union to 400,000 members and taken the field against the intransigent mine owners of Pennsylvania in the first of the decade's climactic labor wars. This occurred in midsummer of 1934, when Lewis called out 70,000 miners to strike.

The companies and their political allies girded for battle. "We're going to meet 'em at the bridge and break their goddam heads," shouted the mayor of Duquesne as the strike spread across the Allegheny Valley. Before it ended, the mine owners had poured some $17,000 into munitions, and their

Armed with billy clubs and auto parts, Chrysler strikers rally beneath a slogan—borrowed from French soldiers—warning scabs to stay away.

henchmen had bombed miners' houses and set crosses ablaze on the hillsides. But in the settlement, the embattled miners won grudging acceptance, and the road toward union recognition was staked out for every man in America's far-flung laboring forces.

With this triumph under his belt, Lewis met with union organizers in Atlantic City, New Jersey, and proposed a drive to pull together all of the country's industrial laborers into an enormous conglomerate. At one point in the maneuvering, Lewis was challenged by a burly trade unionist who called Lewis a "big bastard," to which Lewis replied with a punch in the nose. When the dust of the skirmish had cleared away, a good many of labor's top men had fallen in behind Lewis; the labor conglomerate was formed and subsequently christened the Congress of Industrial Organizations (CIO). Looking back with a certain pleasure on the imbroglios involved, Lewis crowed, "They smote me hip and thigh, and right merrily did I return their blows."

Then he returned to the war with industrial management, this time in Flint, Michigan, home of several General Motors plants. General Motors was then the third-largest corporation in the country. It employed a quarter of a million people, paying its top 20 officials an average of $200,000 a year, its workers scarcely $1,000. It also maintained one of the rankest spy systems in the country; between January 1934 and August 1936 the company paid $994,855.68 to Pinkerton and others.

On December 28, 1936, a thousand workers at one of GM's Cleveland plants, demanding the right to make every GM worker a member of the United Automobile Workers (UAW), adopted a somewhat new and disconcertingly effective tactic. They laid down their tools and went on a sit-down strike; instead of walking out, as most earlier strikers had done, they remained in the plant. Management was stunned. Two days later the night shift at GM's key Chevrolet plant in Flint sat down too. Fifteen more plants followed, stripping General Motors of 140,000 employees and bringing all auto production to a halt.

Sit-down strikers take it easy on assembly-line auto seats inside the Fisher Body plant in Flint, Michigan, during the crucial strike of 1937 (left).

Goons hired by Ford (left) stalk unionists Walter Reuther and Richard Frankensteen.

Surrounding Frankensteen, they grab him and slug him for handing out union leaflets.

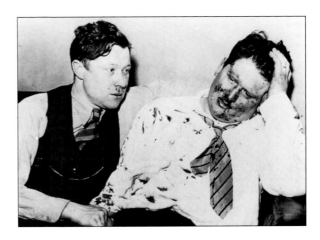

Afterward, Reuther attempts to comfort Frankensteen, who was bloodied in the brawl.

As news of the strikers' victory comes, a jubilant Ladies Auxiliary parades in front of the Chrysler works just before the sit-downers emerge.

The focal point of the conflict was at Flint. As the sit-down continued, the temperature dropped below zero. General Motors officials turned off the heat in the plant and directed the Flint police to seize food bound for the shivering strikers. Some 50 policemen sprayed the pickets with buckshot and tear gas and beat them with clubs. "We wanted peace. General Motors chose war. Give it to them!" shouted a voice over a loudspeaker, and the strikers did, with pipes, door hinges, coffee mugs, pop bottles, and an icy blast from the company's fire hose. After an all-night battle in which 14 men were wounded, the strikers succeeded in routing the police.

Governor Frank Murphy, who had given grueling hours to patient mediation and was determined to keep Michigan from further bloodshed, alerted the National Guard. But he decided to consult with Lewis before sending the men into action. What would Lewis do if the guard tried to evict the strikers? Murphy wanted to know.

"You want my answer, sir?" asked Lewis. "I give it to you. Tomorrow morning, I shall personally enter General Motors plant Chevrolet No. 4. I shall order the men to disregard your order. I shall then walk up to the largest window in the plant, open it, divest myself of my outer raiment, remove my shirt and bare my bosom. Then when you order your troops to fire, mine will be the first those bullets will strike. And as my body falls from that window to the ground, you listen to the voice of your grandfather as he whispers in your ear, 'Frank, are you sure you are doing the right thing?'" Murphy, whose grandfather had been hanged in the Irish rebellion, tore up his order, forbade General Motors to bar the delivery of food to the strikers, and with great tact held further violence at bay.

After 44 days of losing profits at the rate of one million dollars a day, General Motors capitulated, agreeing to bargain with the United Automobile Workers in the 17 plants that had been struck. In four months' time the UAW had won its drive for acceptance and organized a majority of General Motors workers. The strikers had scored a monumental triumph against the third-mightiest corporation in the country. In the wake of that victory labor's final battles for union recognition got under way *(pages 128-133).*

Everybody Sits

With the success of the big strikes, people all over sat down to protest grievances.

When they tie the can to a union man,
Sit down! Sit down!
When they give him the sack they'll take him
*   back,*
Sit down! Sit down!
When the speed-up comes, just twiddle your
*   thumbs,*
Sit down! Sit down!
When the boss won't talk, don't take a walk,
Sit down! Sit down!
—Union ballad

Striking chefs at the Willard Hotel in Washington, D.C., stage their sit-down on top of a cold stove.

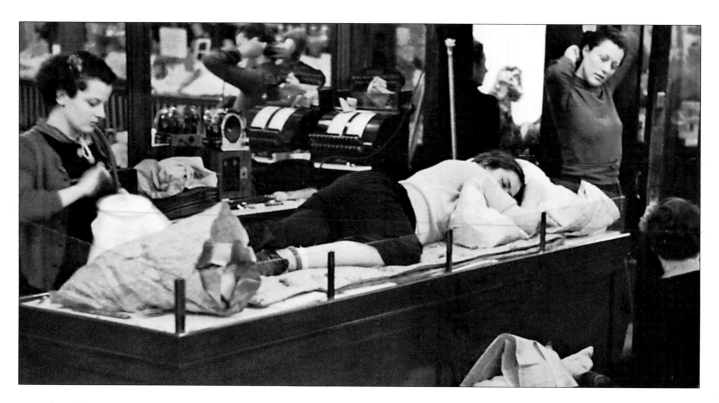

A Woolworth's clerk naps on a counter during a sit-in at Detroit in 1937.

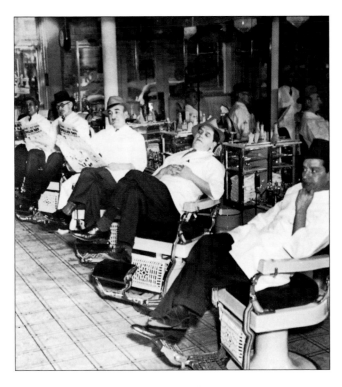

New Jersey barbers sit in a nonunion shop.

Philadelphia hosiery workers awaken a sleeping colleague with the happy news that their strike is won.

An Illinois driver demands that the road be fixed. "I've been stuck here 32 times," he declared.

Striking seamen lounge in deck chairs aboard the SS President Roosevelt en route to Hamburg.

The Hard Grip of Steel

While the nation's eyes were still fixed on the union coup in the automobile industry at Detroit, labor's eloquent leader, John L. Lewis, got busy elsewhere. He took on, virtually single handed, the Goliath of American industry: United States Steel, an antagonist beside which even General Motors seemed comparatively small.

Despite the hard times of the Depression, U.S. Steel, grandly called the Corporation by its officers, reported gross earnings of $35,218,359 in 1934. It turned out more than 53 million tons of iron ore, coal, coke, limestone, pig iron, ingots, and finished steel items, and more than a quarter of a million tons of by-products from ammonia to cement. It owned not only mills but coal and iron mines stretching from Canada to Brazil, a fleet of ships, and miles of railroad tracks to move its cargo.

But the view from inside the mills and mines, the view of the common laborer, was grim and hopeless. In 1933, more than half the mill hands were totally unemployed, and by the Corporation's own statement there was not a single full-time worker anywhere on its payroll. Conditions elsewhere in the steel industry were much the same. That year the average steelworker, with his part-time pickings, earned $369, a sum on which he had to support a family that averaged 5.92 persons. "Work two days a week," said a steelworker in Braddock, Pennsylvania, "loaf around five days, wife sick, one of my girls needs a good doctor, and me with no money, a bunch of rent bills, butcher bills, grocery bills."

Safety conditions were as bad as wages. Occupational diseases such as carbon monoxide poisoning, "hot mill cramps" (from exposure to temperatures up to 220°F at the furnace mouth), and pneumonia took hundreds of lives every year. Every week, on the average, one man could expect his clothes to catch fire, and if he did not burn to death he had to replace the clothes from his meager earnings. The overseer who went by the title of safety manager at a Jones & Laughlin steel mill in Pittsburgh admitted to having "a lot of equipment that is out of date, lacks the new safety devices and is liable to break down at any time, causing serious accidents," but he had no plans for improving it. "It still yields a return on investment," he said, "so the company cannot scrap it." Instead the industry scrapped 22,845 human beings in accidents in a single year: Two hundred forty-two were killed, 1,193 were permanently disabled, and 21,410 were temporarily laid up.

"A world without policemen would be like a world without music."

Daniel J. Shields, mayor of Johnstown, Pennsylvania

Strikers support a coworker who was tear-gassed during one of many protests against steel companies in 1937.

Cartoonist William Gropper bitterly caricatured the repressions of the Chicago steel magnates against workers who struck in the spring of 1937.

CHICAGO

As top dog in the industry, U.S. Steel was habitually followed by its pack of friendly competitors in all matters from wage rates to safety measures and, of course, in its attitude toward unions. On that score, Bethlehem, Republic, Youngstown, National, and Inland—nicknamed Little Steel to differentiate them from the grandiose Corporation—shot down unions with a vigor that would have warmed the hearts of the tough old magnates who laid the foundations of U.S. Steel.

In 1935 Carnegie Steel was paying likely finks about $25 a month to report on union talk among their fellow workers, filing the results of their pickings and firing offenders. Yet Tom M. Girdler, one-time policeman for Jones & Laughlin, now head of Republic Steel, could accuse union organizers of "interference in a man's private affairs." He added, "An ominous fact was repeated in the sketchy facts we had about some of these fellows: They were Communists."

There were some unions in the steel industry, but they were company unions, organizations controlled not by the workers but by management. A Ukrainian mill hand testified at a government investigation of the company union at the Carnegie Steel plant in Duquesne: "Boss say, 'Better you go vote now.' No, I say, I got outside union. I vote in outside union. Boss say then, 'You no like job, huh? No like company? Well, maybe company no like you. Better you go vote now.' "

In all, the steelworkers seemed helpless to improve their lot. But the momentum of the big union victories in coal and autos provided fresh hope; and help was on the way as John L. Lewis, now head of the Congress of Industrial Organizations (CIO), stepped forward as the steelworkers' spokesman. By organizing coal, he had tied up the source of the fuel on which the steel industry ran; by organizing automobiles, he had tied up steel's major customer. Now he turned to U.S. Steel, certain that if he could move the mighty Corporation, its confreres in Little Steel would come along. "If we can organize here," he said, "the rest will follow. If the crouching lion can be routed, it is a safe bet that the hyenas in the adjacent bush may be scattered along the plain."

Lewis was, as a reporter of the day remarked, "a foeman worthy of U.S. Steel." Calling personally on Myron Taylor, the courtly board chairman of the Corporation, he chatted amiably of Gothic tapestries and high finance. Taylor was charmed, and to the nation's astonishment, he

A fallen worker gets a merciless beating as strikers fight scabs during a 1937 strike at Republic Steel in Cleveland (left). Eighteen workers lost their lives.

signed a contract with the CIO union. After 50 years of losing to clubs and gunfire, the steelworkers seemed to have won the war with Lewis's mellifluous words. Unhappily, peace in the industry was still some distance away, for the "hyenas in the adjacent bush" were not so easily scattered. Two months after the U.S. Steel settlement, Little Steel had not budged toward any settlement with the CIO. On May 26, 70,000 workers walked out of 27 plants belonging to Little Steel in seven states, and the companies countered with the bloodiest antiunion battle of the decade.

On Memorial Day some 1,500 workers with their wives and children gathered for a demonstration of solidarity outside the Republic plant in South Chicago. "CIO! Let's go! CIO! Let's go!" they chanted. A corps of 150 Chicago police stormed them with tear gas, night sticks, and 200 rounds of gunfire. "Stand back, you son of a bitch," said one of the cops, "or I will fill you full of lead." Over the next few minutes, in a bloodbath that came to be called the Memorial Day Massacre, the police killed 10 demonstrators and wounded more than 100 others.

"There can be no pity for a mob," said Republic president Tom M. Girdler later, as if to excuse the violence. "As that artistic brawler, Benvenuto Cellini, said," he went on, "'blows are not dealt by measure.' Some of the mob were clubbed after they had started to run from the wrath they had aroused. Some women were knocked down. The policemen were there performing a hazardous and harsh duty. What were women doing there?"

The Little Steel strike lasted two months, and this time the laborers lost. Vigilantes lined up against the strikers, the National Guard was called in to back up management, and the various companies in Little Steel maintained a united front. The workers were up against too much. Exhausted and hungry, they went back to work in July without winning their union.

The loss of the Little Steel strike was a bitter blow to workers everywhere after the heady victories that had gone before it. But it proved to be only a temporary setback. Senator Robert M. La Follette Jr. of Wisconsin launched investigations that exposed the tactics used to crush the Little Steel strike and others, with the result that public opinion began to change and industrial espionage and the sicking of armed guards on factory workers began to disappear. The antiunion shock troops of the Pinkertons turned to private-eye work, and Pearl Bergoff and his goons went out of business.

As Lewis surveyed the scene when the '30s drew to a close, he could mark off the worst hurdles as crossed. Despite the stubborn resistance that still lingered in Little Steel, despite confrontations elsewhere in industry, labor in the main had won its quest for recognition. The cost had been heavy; it had entailed the calling of 22,658 strikes in that single decade, the loss of scores of lives, and the infliction of uncounted injuries. But by the end of 1937, unions had recruited 7.7 million workers who won contracts guaranteeing wages, hours, and safety measures in every kind of company. To the millions of American workers who were mute and hogtied at the outset of the decade, Lewis's eloquent voice had given the power of speech. At one point Lewis even went so far as to administer a landmark scolding over nationwide radio to the president of the United States. During the Little Steel strike a reporter asked President Roosevelt for his views on the stalemate. "A plague o' both your houses," cried FDR in exasperation, echoing the Shakespearean invocations of labor's champion.

Lewis was not amused, and gave vent to his anger in characteristic fashion. "It ill behooves one who has supped at labor's table and who has been sheltered in labor's house," he roared over a network broadcast, "to curse with equal fervor and fine impartiality both labor and its adversaries when they become locked in deadly embrace."

Roosevelt heard Lewis loud and clear, and so did the rest of the nation. For by the end of this bloody decade American workers, once scattered and beaten by the industrial goons, ignored or opposed by politicians, had assumed their rightful places as first-class citizens.

The long war for union recognition nearly over, a California laborer proudly displays his union membership book after a strike in November 1938.

Swing

★

AMERICA GETS IN THE GROOVE

Two swing musicians receive top billing on a Broadway marquee.

The Big Bands Break Loose

Before dawn one cold day in 1938, hundreds of teenagers started lining up in front of New York City's Paramount Theater, literally spilling out onto the street and stopping traffic. A special squad of cops was called to contain the "riot." The riot outside was nothing compared with the one that soon broke loose inside. When the early-morning movie was over, a band on an elevating platform rose out of the orchestra pit; 3,000 adolescents screamed and, as the musicians opened up, began to dance in the aisles. The band was Benny Goodman's, and the music he was playing was "swing."

In the closing years of the decade, all of America was swept by swing fever. In little towns girls in loose skirts and saddle shoes tripped into ice-cream parlors with their boyfriends, plugged nickels into the jukebox, and set the place rocking with their intricate jitterbug dance steps. Radio audiences clustered around their sets to hear their favorite bands *(pages 138-139)* on weekly programs, and on Saturdays they tuned in *Your Hit Parade* to learn the top 10 hits of the week. The *New York Times* solemnly suggested that the craze was getting out of hand, quoting a psychologist on the "dangerously hypnotic influence of swing, cunningly devised to a faster tempo than seventy-two bars to the minute—faster than the human pulse."

Actually, swing was nothing more than jazz under a new name. Black groups in the '20s had developed jazz, which was characterized by a driving rhythm and improvised solos; but few white people heard anything except tame orchestrated versions of it. During the Depression authentic jazz went underground. The record industry almost died out. Many jazz musicians found jobs playing bland music in radio studios. Then, in 1934, 24-year-old Benny Goodman formed a band to play the real jazz to mass audiences. The band's first cross-country tour in 1935 was a string of disasters. By the time the group reached California, it had returned to playing innocuous dance music. At the end of an evening at the Palomar Ballroom in Hollywood, however, Goodman told his sidemen to swing for one set to close the evening. The audience went wild. After that, the swinging sound took the country by storm, and within months this revived form of jazz passed into the mainstream of American culture.

"It makes no diff'rence if it's sweet or hot, just give that rhythm ev'rything you got. Oh, it don't mean a thing, if it ain't got that swing."

"It Don't Mean a Thing," by Irving Mills and Duke Ellington

Teenagers jitterbug their way through 1937's popular Big Apple (opposite). Such dancers, showing off for the crowd, were known as shiners.

The Leaders

Big bands became big business in the late '30s, and their leaders were as famous as movie stars. In fact, many bandleaders made full-length movies. Benny Goodman appeared in *The Big Broadcast of 1937;* Bob Crosby was featured in *Let's Make Music.* As with other celebrities, lives of the big-band leaders became fair game for gossipmongers. When the hot-tempered musical brothers Tommy and Jimmy Dorsey feuded over the proper tempo for a song in 1935 and split up the Dorsey Brothers Orchestra, the story was big news. Another hot item was the marriage of bandleader Kay Kyser to his svelte blonde vocalist, Georgia Carroll. Equally well known among musicians and fans was the notorious Goodman "ray," or stare; Benny Goodman was a perfectionist, and if he turned his ray on an underrehearsed musician, the man's days with the band were considered numbered.

The most dedicated swing fans followed the exploits of their heroes in *Downbeat* and *Metronome,* the trade journals of the popular band musicians. Every year both magazines asked readers to write in the names of their favorite bands. The two polls made a distinction between "sweet" bands, which played the schmaltzy sound popularized by the likes of Guy Lombardo, and swing bands, those with a hard-driving beat and improvised solos. The men at right were the top 10 swing bandleaders of 1939 as selected in *Metronome.*

Benny Goodman

Metronome's top bandleader, the clarinet-playing Goodman was celebrated as the King of Swing.

Tommy Dorsey

After breaking with his brother Jimmy, trombonist Tommy created a new band with a brassier sound.

Artie Shaw

Shaw, though not as hot a clarinetist as Goodman, had a band many fans rated as swinging as Benny's.

Bob Crosby

Bing's kid brother, Bob Crosby, sang with the Dorseys before he left to lead a popular Dixieland band.

Glenn Miller

An excellent arranger, trombonist Glenn Miller played music noted for fast tempos and lead clarinets.

Jimmy Dorsey

Playing both alto sax and clarinet, Jimmy wavered between Dixieland and the more modern swing sound.

Jimmy Lunceford

Lunceford's group was one of the decade's most dynamic bands, with its showmanship and bouncy beat.

Count Basie

Basie's 15-man band featured great vocalists like Jimmy Rushing and the Count's own droll piano style.

Harry James

At first a trumpet soloist with Goodman, James started his own group in 1939—with Benny's backing.

Duke Ellington

A gifted composer, the Duke created a sophisticated style using a jazz sound he called "jungle music."

Martha Tilton
*Known as "Liltin'
Martha Tilton," she
made "And the Angels
Sing" a hit record in
1939 with Benny
Goodman.*

Helen O'Connell
*Famous as Jimmy
Dorsey's canary, swing
fans voted her the top
female vocalist of 1940,
when she was 20.*

Billie Holiday
*The great jazz vocalist
Billie Holiday was almost
unknown when she joined
the Artie Shaw Orchestra
in 1938.*

Canaries and Hits

Almost all the big bands, swing and sweet alike, featured vocalists, usually female. The hot voices—or cool looks—of these singers (aficionados called them canaries) often outdid the orchestras in putting across hit tunes. Above is a lineup of canaries of the late '30s and at right are box scores from the entertainment newspaper *Variety* of the top 15 tunes from 1936 to 1940. As the charts show, many of the most popular songs of the swing age were not strictly swing.

1936

All My Eggs in One Basket
Alone
Chapel in the Moonlight
Did I Remember?
Is It True What They Say
  About Dixie?
It's a Sin to Tell a Lie
Lights Out
Moon Over Miami
The Music Goes 'Round
  and 'Round
On the Beach at Bali Bali
Pennies From Heaven
Red Sails in the Sunset
The Way You Look Tonight
When Did You Leave Heaven?
When I'm With You

1937

Boo Hoo
Chapel in the Moonlight
Harbor Lights
It Looks Like Rain
Little Old Lady
Moonlight and Shadows
My Cabin of Dreams
Once in a While
Sailboat in the Moonlight
September in the Rain
So Rare
That Old Feeling
Vieni Vieni
When My Dreamboat
  Comes Home
You Can't Stop Me
  From Dreaming

Marion Hutton
Blonde Marion Hutton was a vocalist for Glenn Miller. At this time her sister, Betty Hutton, was also a singer.

Ella Fitzgerald
Discovered in an amateur show at age 17, Ella joined Chick Webb and dazzled fans with "A-Tisket A-Tasket."

Mildred Bailey
Singing ballads such as "Willow Weep for Me," Mildred was the top attraction for her husband Red Norvo's band.

1938

Alexander's Ragtime Band
A-Tisket A-Tasket
Bei Mir Bist Du Schön
Cathedral in the Pines
Heigh-Ho
I've Got a Pocketful of Dreams
Love Walked In
Music, Maestro, Please!
My Reverie
Rosalie
Says My Heart
Thanks for the Memory
There's a Gold Mine in the Sky
Ti-Pi-Tin
Whistle While You Work

1939

And the Angels Sing
Beer Barrel Polka
Deep in a Dream
Deep Purple
Jeepers Creepers
Man With the Mandolin
Moon Love
My Prayer
Over the Rainbow
Penny Serenade
Sunrise Serenade
Three Little Fishies
Umbrella Man
Wishing
You Must Have Been
   a Beautiful Baby

1940

Blueberry Hill
Careless
Ferryboat Serenade
God Bless America
I'll Never Smile Again
In an Old Dutch Garden
Indian Summer
Make Believe Island
Oh Johnny
Only Forever
Playmates
Scatterbrain
South of the Border
When You Wish Upon a Star
Woodpecker Song

Hepcats and Swinging Dances

Praise Allah, Wiggle, wiggle, wiggle— / Praise Allah, Wiggle and dance; / Do that stomp with lots of pomp and sweet romance! / Big Apple, Big Apple . . ." Lee David and John Redmond conjured up these lyrics in 1937 for a swing dance that quickly became a national craze: the Big Apple. Although the Big Apple remained a total mystery to conservative adults, they nonetheless did their solemn best to try to explain it *(excerpt below)*. No doubt, the song lyrics on page 145 were just as mystifying. But what truly separated the ickies from the hepcats was the language they spoke *(overleaf)*.

Danced in a circle by a group, the Big Apple is led by one who calls the steps, as in a Virginia reel. Fundamental step is a hop similar to the Lindy Hop. In the words of "Variety," "it requires a lot of floating power and fannying." In groups or singly, the dancers follow the caller and combine such steps as the Black Bottom, "shag," Suzi-Q, Charleston, "truckin'," as well as old square-dance turns like London Bridge, and a formation which resembles an Indian Rain Dance. The Big Apple invariably ends upon a somewhat reverent note, with everybody leaning back and raising his arms heavenward. This movement is called "Praise Allah." Through it all, the "caller" shouts continuously—"Truck to the right . . . Reverse it . . . To the left . . . Stomp that right foot . . . Swing it."
—*Time* magazine, 1937

Completely swept up by the beat of the Big Apple, an adolescent firmly plants her saddle shoes in a spraddle-legged maneuver called Posin'.

Jive Talk

The fast-moving world of swing gave birth to a language called jive that was as free and impressionistic and, to the uninitiated, as confusing as the music itself. Below is an abridged dictionary of this lingo.

Alligator: a devotee of swing.

Canary: a girl vocalist.

Cats: musicians in a swing orchestra.

Corn, mickey mouse, schmaltz, sweet: uninspired music good only for sedate dancing.

Cuttin' a rug: dancing to swing music.

Disc or platter: a recording.

Eighty-eight or mothbox: a piano.

Hepcat: a very knowledgeable swing fan.

Hide or skins: drums, played by a skin-beater.

Ickie: a person who does not understand swing.

In the groove: carried away by swing.

Jam session: informal gathering at which swing musicians play for their own pleasure.

Jitterbug: a dancer responding to swing music.

Kicking out: being very free, improvising.

Knocked out: to be so engrossed as to blot out all else; a superlative of *sent*, which means to be aroused by the music.

Licorice stick: a clarinet.

Long hair: in general, an unaware person; musically, one who prefers symphonic music.

One-nighter: a one-night engagement, often with low, or coffee-and-cake, wages.

Paper man: a musician who plays by the spots (notes) and is unable to improvise.

Plumbing: a trumpet, played by a liver-lips.

Scat singer: a vocalist who substitutes nonsense syllables for words.

Swing: unrestrained but melodic big-band jazz with a strong element of improvisation.

Lindy hoppers kick out

Fats Waller hits the mothbox

Picking a platter to spin

Canaries all: the Andrews Sisters

Cats jam with Duke Ellington around an eighty-eight

Skin-beater Gene Krupa pounds out the rhythm

A knocked-out alligator

Cuttin' a rug

Schmaltzmen play for ickies

Hepcat in the groove

Silly Senders

In the '30s, a spate of nonsense songs swept the country. Some, like the bestsellers below, had lyrics so obscure that many fans never did catch on, and they simply faked the words.

Tutti Frutti

Be a rooty-tooty;
Find yourself a cutie,
Why should you be snooty.
Just take your cutie, sweet patootie,
While you have a Tut-ti Frut-ti.
Go to the nearest Sugar Bowl,
Do yourself a favor.
Get a taste of what I mean
S'got the mostest, bestest flavor.
Tut-ti Frut-ti Frut-ti
Tut-ti Frut-ti Frut-ti
Tut-ti Frut-ti Frut-ti

Three Little Fishies

Down in de meddy in a itty bitty poo,
Fam fee itty fitty and a mama fitty, foo.
"Fim," fed de mama fitty, "fim if oo tan,"
And dey fam and dey fam all over de dam.
Boop boop dit-tem dat-tem what-tem Chu!
Boop boop dit-tem dat-tem what-tem Chu!
Boop boop dit-tem dat-tem what-tem Chu!
And dey fam all over de dam.

The Flat Foot Floogee

There's a new killer diller
There's a new Harlem thriller
A new way to ruin the rugs
A new dance for Jitter Bugs.
The Flat Foot Floogee with the Floy Floy
The Flat Foot Floogee with the Floy Floy
The Flat Foot Floogee with the Floy Floy
Floy Doy, Floy Doy, Floy Doy, Floy Doy;
The Flat Foot Floogee with the Flou Flou
The Flat Foot Floogee with the Flou Flou
The Flat Foot Floogee with the Flou Flou,
Flou Dow, Flou Dow, Flou Dow, Flow Dow.
© 1938, 1966 JEWEL MUSIC

Left, Right and Center

RADICAL REMEDIES FOR ALL WOES

A comrade reads the Sunday Worker in Communist headquarters in New York.

The Panacea Seekers

With capitalism apparently collapsed around its feet and its traditional leaders and formulas wiped out, a sizable segment of the country was frantically seeking new ways of doing things. The quest was reflected in the letters full of plans for beating the Depression that poured onto FDR's desk. A surprising majority of them shared a basic premise: that the United States had a marvelous productive system just aching to create abundance for all. What had to be changed were the financial and political institutions that somehow clogged this horn of plenty.

Thus the search for a remedy to the country's problem started as a kind of innocent democratic exercise, involving a variety of odd people and odd ideas. In Greenwich Village there was leather-coated engineer Howard Scott proposing, in 1932, a social scheme he called Technocracy that would increase the wealth tenfold by substituting energy units called ergs and joules for dollars and cents. In Royal Oak, Michigan, there was the Reverend Charles E. Coughlin plumping for an inflationary, silver-backed currency; from the Louisiana bayous Huey Long *(pages 150-151)* was planning to ride into the White House on his "Share Our Wealth" nostrum. In Hollywood and New York there were the earnest intellectuals lapping up, with various degrees of innocence, an even more powerful share-the-wealth concept at Communist-run meetings. In California there was Dr. Francis Townsend, an old frontier doctor who would take care of old people—not to mention the whole economy—by giving each citizen over 60 the sum of $200 monthly to be spent within 30 days.

As the decade wore on, however, the innocence faded and some of the Messiahs appeared in different guises. Coughlin, for one, slid so far to the right that his lectures dealt less with economics than with Jew-baiting. Many others decided that Adolf Hitler was the real Messiah. They closed ranks with the Berlin-directed German-American Bund, aping the Nazis' salute *(right)*, colored shirts, and broad-gauge racism. As for the Communists, their Soviet idols made a 1939 alliance with Hitler—an ideological turnabout that caused massive disillusionment with people's democracy. By decade's end the seeking after panaceas was about over, for it had become clear that there really weren't any. Furthermore, with the economy alive and progressing, the need seemed no longer urgent, and Americans returned to the practice of leaving politics in the traditional hands of Democratic and Republican politicians.

"The Nazi salute is the coming salute for the whole United States."

Fritz Kuhn, president of the German-American Bund, 1938

A German-American Bundist salutes a New Jersey audience at a 1938 Washington's Birthday rally (opposite). Bundists called Washington "the first Fascist."

Huey Long, the cocky governor of Louisiana, had few peers as a campaigner. A tireless handshaker, he also twisted arms when the need arose.

The Pied Piper of the Bayous

Almost everybody outside of Louisiana saw its governor, Huey Long, as the outrageous demagogue and dictator he was. An unabashed egotist who called himself the Kingfish after a pompous radio character of the day, he ran the state with a capricious will backed by the guns of the police. However, to the poor farmers who made up the state's largest bloc of voters, Long was an infallible friend.

Long's mass appeal was based on a dreamy program, to which he gave the alluring name "Share Our Wealth." Theoretically, Huey would take from the rich and give to the poor. In actual practice, he levied many consumer taxes that, as always, hit the poor the hardest; and he increased the state deficit by almost $100 million.

Long also sold himself a dream—that he would become the president of the Yew-nited States. Huey felt so certain of it that he wrote a book entitled *My First Days in the White House*. This arrogant fantasy appears in excerpt below. Unhappily for the Kingfish, his dream would not come true, for he was shot dead by a constituent who could endure no more of Long's predations.

"My worries about the completion of my cabinet being almost over, I . . . set in motion my plan for a redistribution of the nation's wealth."

Huey Long, *My First Days in the White House*, 1935

Soon after I had sent the cabinet names to the Senate, my secretary informed me that Mr. Hoover was trying to get me on the telephone. . . . I heard the voice of that Quaker gentleman say: "Er-r-r-r, Mr. President—er-r-r, this is Hoover. Is it true that you have tendered me the position of Secretary of Commerce?"

I said I had sent his name to the Senate.

"But, Mr. President, I should have been consulted. This has placed me in a very embarrassing position."

"In what way, Mr. Hoover?" I inquired.

"Why, I am a former President of the United States, and it's a terrible step down for me to be asked to serve in your cabinet," he replied.

"Just what is your position in public life today, Mr. Hoover?"

He hesitated and then: "Well, suppose I decline on the ground that I do not care to be associated with you?"

"All right, Mr. Hoover," I replied. "That is something for you to decide in your own conscience."

Mr. Hoover's voice lost its angry tone. "All right, Mr. President," he replied. "I will consider it."

Some minutes after ten o'clock that night I was called to the telephone. I heard a voice: "Hello, Kingfish!"

It was Franklin D. Roosevelt. "Yes, Mr. President," I answered.

"What in the world do you mean by offering me a cabinet post, after all the things you have said about me as President?"

"I only offered you a position which I thought you were qualified to fill."

"Well, it's a terrible fall from the Presidency to the Secretaryship of the Navy," he replied.

"You sound just like Hoover," I said, "but he couldn't call to mind any position he held just now."

"Well, Huey, I'll have to give this more consideration," the former President told me. "I had a statement all prepared here, declining, but I'll destroy it. Say, suppose I accept and fail to become the best Secretary? What's the penalty then?"

"In that case," I replied, "people will hold me responsible, and they may punish me for your failure."

The former President chuckled: "Well, Huey, that's almost reason enough to accept the position. You'll hear from me later."

My worries about the completion of my cabinet being almost over, I undertook to set in motion my plan for a redistribution of the nation's wealth.

—Huey Long, *My First Days in the White House*, 1935

Radio's Political Priest

As a political speaker, Father Charles E. Coughlin was second in popularity only to President Roosevelt. Millions listened to the priest's angry tirades and radical schemes for sharing the wealth, broadcast every Sunday from the Shrine of the Little Flower at Royal Oak, Michigan. In 1934, when Coughlin launched his own party, the National Union for Social Justice, more than five million listeners signed up within two months.

Though Coughlin was "for" social justice, among other causes, he was better known by the things he was against. First and last, he was anti-Communist. He became violently anti-Roosevelt, calling the president a "great betrayer" because the New Deal allegedly had "communistic tendencies." Coughlin made anti-Semitic remarks about "the Jewish bankers," and he also attacked both the labor unions and the industrial capitalists.

These extreme views were met by a rising storm of protest. Under pressure from all quarters, Coughlin slowly curtailed his political activities; and by mid-1940 the air ceased to crackle with fulminations such as those excerpted below.

"We cannot applaud a New Deal . . . with all its chaotic implications. . . ."

Father Charles E. Coughlin, March 1935

President Roosevelt has both compromised with the money changers and conciliated with monopolistic industry. This spirit of compromise has been the predominant weakness of our present leadership to such an extent that it has not disdained to hold out the olive branch to those whose policies are crimsoned with the theories of sovietism and international socialism.

We cannot applaud a New Deal which, with all its chaotic implications, submits either to the supremacy of a financial overlord more obnoxious than King George III or to the red slavery of an economic Simon Legree.
—March 1935

As far as the National Union is concerned, no candidate which is endorsed for Congress can campaign, go electioneering for, or support the great betrayer and liar, Franklin D. Roosevelt, he who promised to drive the money changers from the temple and succeeded in driving the farmers from their homesteads and the citizens from their homes in the cities.

He who promised to drive the money changers from the temple has built up the greatest debt in history, $35,000,000,000, which he permitted the bankers the right, without restriction, to spend, and for which he contracted that you and your children shall repay with seventy billion hours of labor.

I ask you to purge the man who claims to be a Democrat from the Democratic party, and I mean Franklin Double-Crossing Roosevelt.
—July 1936

When any upstart dictator in the U.S. succeeds in making this a one party form of government, when the ballot is useless, I shall have the courage to stand up and advocate the use of bullets. Mr. Roosevelt is a radical. The Bible commands "increase and multiply," but Mr. Roosevelt says to destroy and devastate. Therefore I call him anti-God.
—September 1936

If we are sincere, we will recall all the Ambassadors and Ministers from the communist countries, from Mexico, from Barcelona, in whose suburbs 300 innocent nuns—the breath of life still in their bodies—were drenched with kerosene and burned.

I say to the good Jews of America, be not indulgent with the irreligious, atheistic Jews and Gentiles who promote the cause of persecution in the land of the Communists, the same ones who promote the cause of atheism in America. Yes, be not lenient with your high financiers and politicians who assisted at the birth of the only . . . system in all civilization that adopted atheism as its religion . . . and slavery as its liberty.
—November 1938

Father Charles E. Coughlin carries the political battle to his many enemies. Later he admitted, "It was a horrible mistake to enter politics."

Communist leader Mother Bloor, shown with beauty-contest winners, was prized by Reds for her deep-dish American look and colonial forebears.

CLUB BARRON

YCL

YOUNG COMMUNIST LEAGUE

The Very Red-Blooded Americans

In 1937 the New York chapter of the Daughters of the American Revolution (DAR) unaccountably failed to celebrate the 162nd anniversary of Paul Revere's ride. On the appointed day, however, hooves clattered along Broadway, and into view cantered a horse with a rider attired in Continental costume. He carried a sign: "The DAR forgets but the YCL remembers." The YCL stood for the Young Communist League, and the incident stood for the zany fact that between 1935 and 1939, nobody worked harder at being American than the American Communists. They tried to build an image of the party as a native American organization, made up of just plain folks who were anxious to cooperate with other patriots. Explained a YCL leaflet at the University of Wisconsin: "Some people have the idea that a YCLer is politically minded, that nothing outside of politics means anything. Gosh no. We go to shows, parties and all that. The YCL and its members are no different from other people."

The sudden transformation of the local Bolsheviks into 200 percent Americans began in 1935 in, of all places, Moscow. Realizing that Hitler meant one day to attack Russia, the Soviets shelved their traditional anticapitalist dogma and ordered Communists the world over to form the widest possible alliances to protect the motherland. The new line was called the Popular Front, and the U.S. party skillfully carried it out. Donning a cheerful, homespun exterior and waving the American flag, Communists trotted out such respectable symbols as Ella Reeves "Mother" Bloor, daughter of a Republican banker, to give themselves a flavor of old-established Americanism and to help woo others with WASP names and Mayflower lineages. New York units joined black churches in organizing Mother's Day observances, and the *Daily Worker* inaugurated a super-American sports section.

Different organizations called fronts were set up to attract ordinary Americans of every persuasion. Fronts were established to further the interests of medical interns, folk singers, theater buffs, book-club joiners, and so on. At their peak, the fronts had more than seven million members, represented over 1,000 affiliated organizations, and had acquired a certain respectability. The 1939 congress of the American League against War and Fascism was welcomed in Washington both by the secretary of the interior and the Grand Exalted Ruler of the Elks.

Hollywood was where the Popular Front really kicked up dust. After studio hours Beverly Hills buzzed with activities for a variety of causes, some of enduring value: the Hollywood Anti-Nazi League, the Screen Writers' Guild, the Theatre Committee for the Defense of the Spanish Republic. Stars threw open their hearts, homes, and swimming pools so that Hollywood's Popular Front offered an irresistible bargain—an opportunity to combine social climbing with do-gooding. Where else could liberals rub shoulders with the likes of Myrna Loy, Edward G. Robinson, and James Cagney? The film community enjoyed being involved with real history and gave generously of time and money. Benefits for the Abraham Lincoln Brigade *(overleaf)*, a group of Americans who volunteered to fight in the Spanish Civil War, never yielded less than $5,000 to $8,000. And once, when the editor of the Communist magazine *New Masses* appealed for funds at a bigwig's home, he came away with $20,000.

It was fun while it lasted. But on August 23, 1939, in another spectacular about-face, Russia signed with Germany the Nazi-Soviet pact and Stalin toasted Hitler's health: "I know how much the German nation owes to its Fuehrer." At that shocking piece of double-think, the ideological ground beneath the Popular Front gave way, and it soon collapsed. Within a few months the American Communist Party lost thousands of members, especially among the intellectuals, and many thousands of other Americans who had been pursuing good causes under a Red banner awoke to the realization that they'd been had.

The End of a Crusade

When the Fascist General Francisco Franco, supported by both Hitler and Mussolini, marched to overthrow Spain's Republican Government, idealistic Americans sided strongly with the Republicans. More than 3,000 American men went to Spain to fight in a volunteer unit called the Abraham Lincoln Brigade. Below are excerpts from the letters home of one volunteer, Wilfred Mendelson of Brooklyn, who was killed in action July 28, 1938.

June 3, 1938
I am writing from the training base of the Spanish People's Army. Last night we marched into the nearby town. The older women, careworn faces, thinking of their own sons and husbands at the front, cried. The young girls smiled or raised arms in the popular salute. Our 4,000-mile journey was being understood, appreciated.

June 5, 1938
Sunday in Spain. It is very quiet, almost blissful.

June 22, 1938
About myself, I am doing fine, a good shot really, like a Coney Island range expert. This summer may well seal the fate of world peace. Everybody must be brought to the realization that every day Spain continues in its efforts time is gained for the peace forces all over. In this light Spain is holding the fort for America. If America does not rally it is cutting its own throat.

July 15, 1938
I've seen a magnificent cathedral rising through Barcelona completely stripped of interior and exterior. But that can convey nothing to me. My brain says "Bombers", I know it, I see it, but the terror just isn't there.

July 23, 1938
Looks like any hour now we'll be off. While our forces are tremendously strong and we confidently expect victory, accidents do happen to individuals. Don't show this note to my parents. Take care of them. I love you.

Veterans of the Abraham Lincoln Brigade, back home from Spain, give the Popular Front clenched-fist salute at a 1939 May Day parade.

The Movies

★

HOLLYWOOD RETREATS FROM REALITY

After a Saturday matinee, kids show off their door prizes.

Paradise in Celluloid

No one who spent time at the movies during the '30s would never have known that the nation was down in the dumps. In a typical Hollywood movie of the era, Bette Davis gave up "everything" for the man she loved and moved into a remodeled Vermont farmhouse that one sarcastic critic estimated would cost $12,000 a year just to operate. In other films the vestiges of the real, cruel world of the Depression were replaced by delightful fictions like Walt Disney's 1937 *Snow White and the Seven Dwarfs,* by horror classics like 1931's *Dracula* and 1933's *King Kong,* and by superspectacular musicals such as the 1933 *Flying Down to Rio,* in which a whole chorus of show girls in gauze uniforms dance on the wings of airplanes in flight.

Hollywood's brand of heaven on earth was a deliberate and enormously successful effort to provide escape. Some 85 million people a week seized on it, commonly paying 25 cents for a ticket (10 cents for kids). Local theaters enhanced the appeal of a night at the movies by offering double and even triple features and by giving away door prizes that ranged from coupons for free hairdos to shiny new automobiles. The religion of escape had its icons; Shirley Temple dolls and rubber statuettes of Disney's dwarfs sold in the millions. The high priestess of Hollywood was gossip Louella Parsons, who divulged her "exclusives" every week on her radio show. Every year thousands of pilgrims journeyed to Hollywood to make reverent tours of the homes of the stars.

Not only were American films devoutly escapist, they were also, after 1934, very clean. In that year America's Roman Catholic bishops banded together to form the National League of Decency, and Hollywood cooperated with it by enforcing a long list of taboos. Long kisses, adultery, double beds, words like "damn" and "hell," and even nude babies were banned from films. Criminals could no longer triumph over decent citizens. An actress like Mae West could no longer croon "I Like a Man Who Takes His Time." The day of "family movies" was ushered in, featuring adorable youngsters like Shirley Temple, Mickey Rooney, and Jane Withers. Jeanette MacDonald and Nelson Eddy—whom Hollywood cynics dubbed the Iron Butterfly and the Singing Capon—began to turn out a whole series of fluffy white operettas. Even the titles of motion pictures were cleaned up; thus *Good Girls Go to Paris Too* became *Good Girls Go to Paris,* and *Infidelity,* by a miraculous transformation, turned into *Fidelity.*

"The American film has served as propaganda for the emotional monotony, the naive morality, the sham luxury, the haphazard etiquette and the grotesque exaggeration of the comic, the sentimental and the acrobatic that are so common in the United States."

Poet and critic John Gould Fletcher

Year-by-year charts of the top-10 box-office stars (opposite), begun in 1932 by Motion Picture Herald, show Clark Gable's durability and Shirley Temple's rise and fall.

1932	1933	1934	1935	1936	1937	1938	1939	1940
Marie Dressler	Marie Dressler	Will Rogers	Shirley Temple	Shirley Temple	Shirley Temple	Shirley Temple	Mickey Rooney	Mickey Rooney
Janet Gaynor	Will Rogers	Clark Gable	Will Rogers	Clark Gable	Clark Gable	Clark Gable	Tyrone Power	Spencer Tracy
Joan Crawford	Janet Gaynor	Janet Gaynor	Clark Gable	Astaire-Rogers	Robert Taylor	Sonja Henie	Spencer Tracy	Clark Gable
Charles Farrell	Eddie Cantor	Wallace Berry	Astaire-Rogers	Robert Taylor	Bing Crosby	Mickey Rooney	Clark Gable	Gene Autry
Greta Garbo	Wallace Berry	Mae West	Joan Crawford	Joe E. Brown	William Powell	Spencer Tracy	Shirley Temple	Tyrone Power
Norma Shearer	Jean Harlow	Joan Crawford	Claudette Colbert	Dick Powell	Jane Withers	Robert Taylor	Bette Davis	James Cagney
Wallace Berry	Clark Gable	Bing Crosby	Dick Powell	Joan Crawford	Astaire-Rogers	Myrna Loy	Alice Faye	Bing Crosby
Clark Gable	Mae West	Shirley Temple	Wallace Berry	Claudette Colbert	Sonja Henie	Jane Withers	Errol Flynn	Wallace Berry
Will Rogers	Norma Shearer	Marie Dressler	Joe E. Brown	Jeanette MacDonald	Gary Cooper	Alice Faye	James Cagney	Bette Davis
Joe E. Brown	Joan Crawford	Norma Shearer	James Cagney	Gary Cooper	Myrna Loy	Tyrone Power	Sonja Henie	Judy Garland

Slinky Jean Harlow gazes longingly at herself in Dinner at Eight. Called the Blonde Bombshell, she was the sexiest siren of the early '30s.

The sexiest male, by popular acclaim, was Clark Gable, shown here in his costume for the part of Mr. Christian in Mutiny on the Bounty.

Some connoisseurs of Hollywood beauty preferred the shapely legs of Marlene Dietrich—shown here in Blonde Venus—to Harlow's slithery appeal.

Gary Cooper, all done up for his role in the 1935 thriller *Lives of a Bengal Lancer*, rivaled Gable at the box office as Hollywood's top he-man.

The Versatile Vixen

Very likely the most talented star of the decade was a popeyed little dynamo named Bette Davis. Although her own personality was so strong that every screen character she played, from the Old Maid to Jezebel, was unmistakably Bette Davis, she was nevertheless able to inject a biting realism into a remarkable range of roles. Off screen she was every bit as strong willed and sharp tongued as the characters she played in her films. Her leading man Errol Flynn once commented to her, "I'd love to proposition you, Bette, but I'm afraid you'd laugh at me." Bette responded sweetly, "You're so right, Errol."

Jezebel

Petrified Forest

Dark Victory

Juarez

The Old Maid

Of Human Bondage

Marked Woman

Errol Flynn leers at the Virgin Queen in The Private Lives of Elizabeth and Essex, in which Bette Davis played the 60-year-old monarch.

Sing a Song of Money

In the celluloid paradise created by Hollywood, some of the purest bits of froth were the musicals. These came in several delicious flavors, one fan favorite being the supercolossal productions of Busby Berkeley *(pages 170-171)*, which usually were built around lovebirds Dick Powell and Ruby Keeler. Another sticky-sweet variety featured Jeanette Mac-Donald and Nelson Eddy in schmaltzy operettas.

The biggest moneymakers, however, were Fred Astaire and Ginger Rogers. Before they were teamed up, Ginger had played only a few feature parts. The report on Fred's first Hollywood screen test had read, "Can't act. Slightly bald. Can dance a little." But the first film in which they starred, *The Gay Divorcée* in 1934, turned out to be such a smash that RKO insured Fred's legs for a million dollars. By the end of the decade the team had tapped its way through seven more hits, Astaire was branching out to start a chain of dance studios, and Ginger was striking out on her own as an award-winning dramatic actress.

Nelson Eddy sings with Jeanette MacDonald in Rose Marie.

In the 1938 film Carefree, Fred Astaire and Ginger Rogers perform a step called the Yam, which one magazine suggested fans learn for home parties.

Fiddling fairies swirl in Gold Diggers of 1933. This sequence is typical of the choreography of Busby Berkeley, master of '30s musicals.

Crime Pays

The 1930 crime film *Little Caesar* taught movie producers that multiple murders meant multiple box-office dollars. *Caesar* set off a spate of gangster films whose swaggering stars were accused of schooling a generation of real-life punks. Hollywood, to duck accusations that it was glorifying the underworld, always knocked off the crime lord in the last reel. But censors were unmoved, and films glorifying gangsters died of official disapproval and public boredom.

Bullets slam into Edward G. Robinson as Little Caesar.

Public Enemy James Cagney sells his booze to a bar owner.

Armed with various gifts, Paul Muni (left) as Scarface, accompanied by a henchman played by George Raft, prepare to pay a farewell call on a hospitalized rival.

The Funnymen

Mae West tries her best to look coy as W. C. Fields offers a few sly suggestions in My Little Chickadee, a Western spoof larded with Fieldisms.

My Little Chickadee

During the '30s Hollywood developed the full spectrum of film comedy. The best was the slapstick of the Marx Brothers (pages 176-177) and the low-key love satires like those excerpted here. In a memorable scene from My Little Chickadee, snake-oil peddler Cuthbert J. Twillie (W. C. Fields) chances upon a social outcast named Flower Belle Lee (Mae West).

Fields: *Nice day.*

West: *Is it?*

Fields: *Course it's only one man's opinion. May I present my card?*

West: *Novelties and notions. What kind of notions you got?*

Fields: *You'd be surprised. Some are old, some are new. Whom have I the honor of addressing, my lady?*

West: *Mmmm—they call me Flower Belle.*

Fields: *Flower Belle. What a euphonious appellation—easy on the ears and a banquet for the eyes.*

Carole Lombard, in her pajamas, fends off John Barrymore.

Twentieth Century

On the famous train, Broadway impresario Barrymore meets Carole Lombard, an ex-love he had made a star. He tries to woo her back by outlining a wild religious play in which she will star.

Barrymore: *I'm going to have Judas strangle himself with a hair. I want to stagger New York with 100 camels and real sand—brought from the Holy Land—and we'll have a Babylonian banquet where you're covered with emeralds from head to foot and nothing else. You go directly into your snake dance—it's perfect, but it's nothing compared to the finish, where you stand in rags and the Emperor Nero himself offers you half his empire. The last we see of you is as a pathetic little figure selling olives on the—*
Lombard: *You're craaazzzzy!*

"Flower Belle. What a euphonious appellation—easy on the ears and a banquet for the eyes."

W. C. Fields in *My Little Chickadee*

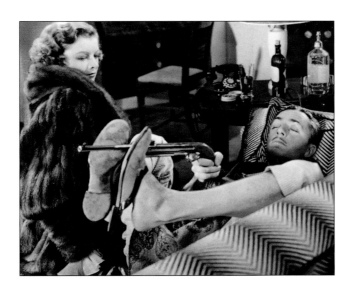

Myrna Loy waits for William Powell to finish target practice.

The Thin Man

Having been tagged as a suspect in a murder, detective Nick Charles (William Powell) swaps bons mots as he toys with the gun he has received as a Christmas present from his wife Nora (Myrna Loy).

Loy: *I'm glad you're not on this case.*
Powell: *The point is, I'm in it. They think I did it.*
Loy: *Well, didn't you?*
(Powell shoots out half a dozen Christmas tree ornaments.)
Loy: *You're not in a shooting gallery. (Picking up a newspaper) Finished with this?*
Powell: *Yes, and I know as much about the murder as they do. So I'm a hero; I was shot twice in the "Tribune."*
Loy: *And I read you were shot five times in the tabloid.*
Powell: *It's not true. He didn't come near my tabloid.*

Esther Muir cringes amid the chaos produced by the Marx Brothers—Groucho (far right), Harpo (center), and Chico—in A Day at the Races.

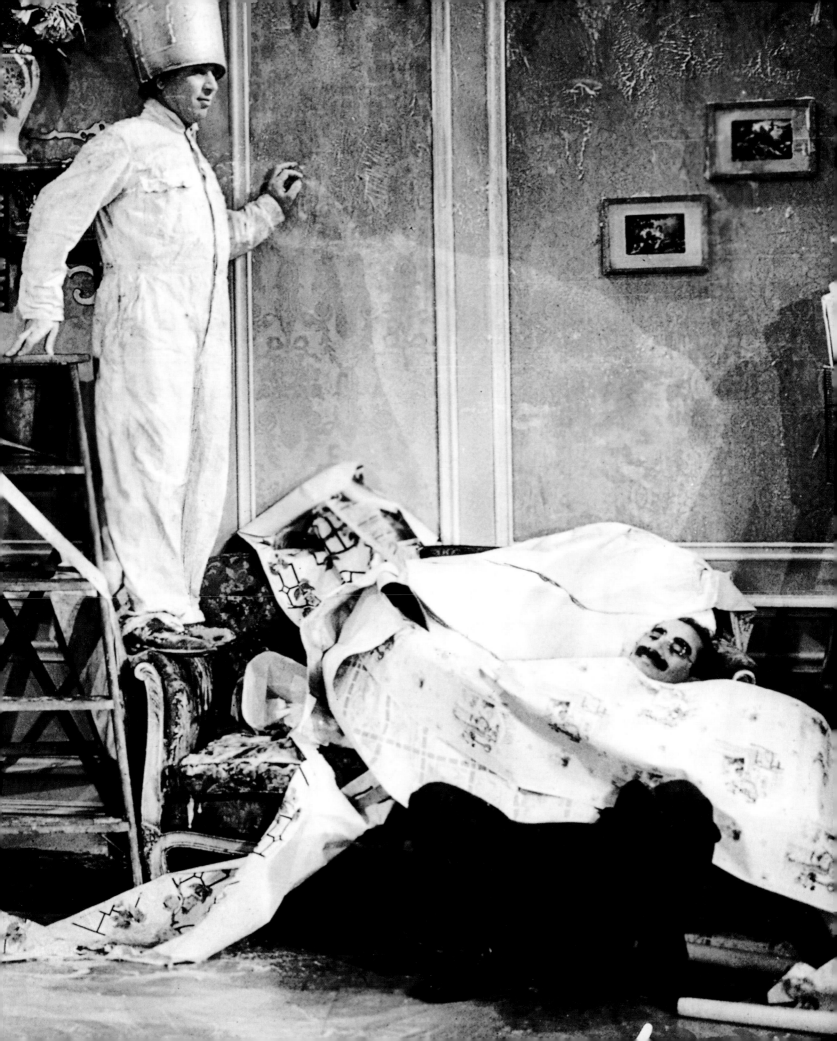

Snow White inspects the dwarfs' hands before dinner.
The leader of the dwarfs was Doc (far left); the
audience favorite was Dopey (far right).

Animated Fantasy

Hollywood's retreat from reality climaxed in Walt Disney's first feature-length cartoon, *Snow White and the Seven Dwarfs.* Disney and his legion of animators started work on the movie in 1934, and for a long time it seemed they might never make it. Financiers were reluctant to lend them the nearly two million dollars they needed. Friends and enemies warned Disney that the public would never pay to sit through an 80-minute fairy tale.

But when the movie was finally unreeled after three years in production, kids of all ages flocked to watch the amiable cavorting of Disney's dwarfs and to swoon over Prince Charming. The movie quickly broke all previous attendance records, grossed eight million dollars, and was translated into 10 languages. Critics, too, were ecstatic, not only about the brilliant animation but also about the musical score (including "Heigh Ho," "Whistle While You Work," and "Some Day My Prince Will Come"). So vivid were some of the sequences that Radio City Music Hall, according to one legend, had to reupholster all the seats after the movie's run; apparently so many children were terrified by Snow White's wicked stepmother that the seats were thoroughly drenched after each performance.

The dwarfs look on as Prince Charming revives Snow White after her stepmother poisons her.

179

Wizard of Oz

Eager to re-create in movies what had succeeded on Broadway, Hollywood in the '30s gobbled up the film rights to old stage musicals. Among these was *The Wizard of Oz,* a hit play based on a children's book by L. Frank Baum in which a tornado whisks a Kansas farm girl named Dorothy to the magic land of Oz.

MGM Studios acquired the rights to the story in 1938, after the success of Disney's *Snow White and the Seven Dwarfs.* Production began within the year. Starring 16-year-old Judy Garland as Dorothy *(right),* the movie also showcased several vaudeville stars, from Broadway headliner Frank Morgan, who played the Wizard, to veteran song-and-dance men Ray Bolger (Scarecrow), Jack Haley (Tin Woodman), and Bert Lahr (Cowardly Lion). Together with a cast of hundreds, including Munchkins, winged monkeys, and witches helpful and wicked, they offered moviegoers at the end of a troubled decade a reassuring tale of good conquering evil, unforgettable songs such as "Somewhere Over the Rainbow," and the heartwarming message that there really is no place like home.

Silver in the children's book, Dorothy's shoes became glittering red in the 1939 MGM film to take full advantage of the relatively new Technicolor system. Shoemakers created several pairs of ruby slippers to allow for the inevitable wear of dancing.

Heroine Scarlett O'Hara, played by English actress Vivien Leigh, savors an embrace with dashing blockade-runner Rhett Butler (Clark Gable) in Gone With the Wind.

Olivia de Havilland as Melanie

Leslie Howard as Ashley

Thomas Mitchell as Mr. O'Hara

Searchlights play on Atlanta's Grand Theater on opening night.

Hattie McDaniel as Mammy

Marching Through Georgia

The most expensive and most discussed movie of the '30s was *Gone With the Wind*. The picture had its premiere on December 15, 1939, in Atlanta, Georgia, the city where much of the film's Civil War action was set. For years people had been awaiting the opening night. Producer David O. Selznick had bought the screen rights to Margaret Mitchell's novel in 1936 and then ballyhooed his project by conducting a nationwide hunt for a new face to play the heroine, Scarlett O'Hara.

About 1,400 actresses were interviewed, and the public wrote in thousands of suggestions. When Vivien Leigh was finally chosen, screams of outrage arose because she was English and not American.

Then came the world premiere. The theater had been rebuilt to resemble a mansion featured in the film, and pretty usherettes wore hoop skirts. And when Miss Leigh appeared on the screen, the old outrage turned to adoration. The feeling quickly spread to the other stars *(above)* and to the show itself. After the show was over, the president-general of the United Daughters of the Confederacy announced, "No one can quarrel now with the selection of Miss Leigh as Scarlett. She is Margaret Mitchell's Scarlett to the life. The whole thing has me overcome."

The Heyday of Horror

First introduced in a feature film in 1927, sound during the '30s did more than give Mae West her purr, the Seven Dwarfs their whistle, and Toto her bark. It resuscitated a mainstay of silent film—the horror movie.

Now terror could be intensified with the creaking of a door, the howling of wolves, or the whistling of wind through Gothic manor towers. Not only did actor Bela Lugosi's vampire look evil in the 1931 movie *Dracula (left)*, but his eerie Hungarian accent sounded villainous as well. Though not visible on screen, bones and skin could be heard crumbling to dust in *The Mummy* (1932), starring Boris Karloff. And the mere sound of Claude Rains's breathing gave away his sinister character's hiding place in *The Invisible Man* (1933). Sound—including the grating of heavy boots on a stone stairway that announced the monster's appearance in *Frankenstein*—made such experiences all the more real, and audiences loved it.

The eight major studios produced about 30 horror films between 1931 and 1936 alone, and dozens more premiered before the end of the decade. Along with those mentioned above, films like *Dr. Jekyll and Mr. Hyde, The Hunchback of Notre Dame, The Old Dark House, Murders in the Rue Morgue, King Kong (overleaf),* and even sequels, notably *The Bride of Frankenstein,* set standards for hair raising and fright inducing that were often imitated but rarely surpassed, making the '30s truly Hollywood's classic age of horror.

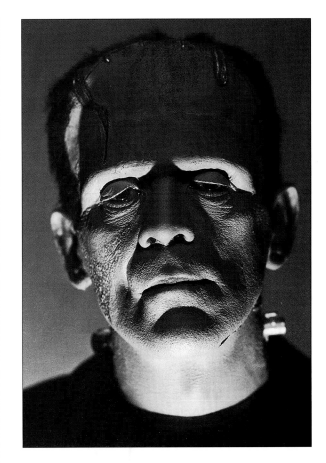

It took four hours to apply the makeup required to transform actor Boris Karloff (above) into the bolt-necked monster-star of the 1931 classic Frankenstein, yet Karloff's face was left basically unencumbered, allowing for a full range of frightening expression.

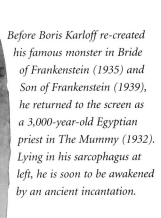

Before Boris Karloff re-created his famous monster in Bride of Frankenstein (1935) and Son of Frankenstein (1939), he returned to the screen as a 3,000-year-old Egyptian priest in The Mummy (1932). Lying in his sarcophagus at left, he is soon to be awakened by an ancient incantation.

Hungarian-born actor Bela Lugosi as Dracula, the Transylvanian vampire, welcomes visitors to his cobweb-infested castle.

Atop the Empire State Building, King Kong clutches an attacking plane and swats at others just before they shoot him in the monster thriller released in 1933.

ACKNOWLEDGMENTS

The editors wish to thank the following individuals and institutions for their valuable assistance in the preparation of this volume:
Forrest J Ackerman, Forrest J Ackerman Archives, Los Angeles; Atlanta Historical Society; A. K. Baragwanath, Senior Curator, Museum of the City of New York; Busby Berkeley, Los Angeles; Larry Booth, Director of Historical Collection, Title Insurance and Trust Company, San Diego; Mrs. Ruth P. Braun, Chief Librarian, *Detroit News;* Mrs. Loraine Burdick, Celebrity Doll Club, Puyallup, Washington; Ted Cavagnaro, St. Louis; Mrs. Shirley Clarke, Curator, Audio-Visual Materials, Labor History Archives, Wayne State University, Detroit; Harry Collins, Brown Brothers; Charles Correll and Freeman Gosden, Los Angeles; Patricia Crews, *Daily Oklahoman,* Oklahoma City; Robert Cunningham, Stillwater, Okla.; Virginia Daiker, Prints and Photographs Division, Library of Congress; James H. Davis, Western History Division, Denver Public Library; Frank Driggs, New York; Cam Duane, Institute of Texan Cultures, San Antonio; Moe Fishman, Secretary, Veterans of the Abraham Lincoln Battalion, New York; Woody Gelman, Nostalgia Press, New York; Dorothy Gimmestad, Assistant Curator, Audio-Visual Library, Minnesota Historical Society, St. Paul; Tony Goodstone, New York; Chester Gould, *Chicago Tribune;* Jim Harmon, Radio Heroes Society, Hollywood, Calif.; Martin Herman, *Philadelphia Bulletin;* Historical Society of Pennsylvania, Philadelphia; Hoblitzelle Theatre Arts Library, University of Texas, Austin; Roy King, Librarian, *St. Louis Post Dispatch;* Walter Kost, Manager, Consumer and Promotion Services, General Mills Inc., Minneapolis; Paul J. McLaughlin, Joseph W. Marshall, Mrs. Clarice D. Morris, Franklin D. Roosevelt Library, Hyde Park, New York; John McCarty, Director, High Plains Art Gallery, Amarillo, Tex.; Garnett McCoy, Archivist, Archives of American Art, Detroit; Herbert McLaughlin, Arizona Photographic Associates, Phoenix; Robert D. Monroe, Director of Special Collections, University of Washington Library, Seattle; Dan Morgenstern, *Down Beat,* Chicago; Sol Novin, Culver Pictures, New York; Francis V. O'Connor, University of Maryland; Edward J. Orth, Los Angeles; Margot P. Pearsall, Curator, Social History Division, Detroit Historical Museum; Warner Pflug, Archivist, Labor History Archives, Wayne State University, Detroit; Victor R. Plukas, Security Pacific National Bank, Los Angeles; Henry Raduta, Manager, Chicago Tribune-New York News Syndicate Inc.; Gleason W. Romer, Miami; Marthanne B. Root, Austin; Sy Seidman, New York; Robert Shipler, Salt Lake City; Mildred Simpson, Librarian, Library of Motion Picture Arts and Sciences, Los Angeles; R. Henderson Shuffler, Director, Institute of Texan Cultures, San Antonio; Ernest Smith, New York; Paul Smith, President, Johnson Smith Company, Grosse Pointe; Ray Stuart, R. R. Stuart Collection, Los Angeles; Patrick Sullivan, Massachusetts State Library, Boston; Judith Topaz, Assistant, Iconographic Collections, State Historical Society of Wisconsin, Madison; Ernest Trova, St. Louis; John Conrad Weiser, New York; Al Williamson, Callicoon, New York; Mrs. Ione Wollenzein, Waukesha, Wis.; Mary Yushak, Museum of Modern Art, New York; Jerome Zerbe, New York.

TEXT CREDITS

25: Will Rogers quote: Will Rogers, *How We Elect Our Presidents,* Donald Day, ed., Little, Brown, 1952, p. 111. **36:** Kaltenborn broadcast from H. V. Kaltenborn, *I Broadcast the Crisis,* New York, Random House, 1938. **39:** "Invasion From Mars" by Howard Koch. Reprinted by permission of author and Manheim Fox Enterprises. 1938, 1940, 1967, 1969 Copyright Howard Koch. **44:** Autoworker quote adapted from *The New Republic,* March 18, 1931, pp. 118-119. **49:** Tennessee squatter quote adapted from *These Are Our Lives,* by the Federal Writers' Project, Works Progress Administration, University of North Carolina Press, 1939, pp. 375-376. **59:** Migratory worker's logbook adapted from *Brother Can You Spare a Dime?* Milton Meltzer, Alfred A. Knopf, 1969, p. 140. **69:** "Little Orphan Annie Song" courtesy of Ovaltine Food Products. **73:** "Have You Tried Wheaties." Lyrics by Donald D. Davis and music by M. K. Jerome. Music copyright 1919 by General Mills, Inc. Copyright renewed 1946. Lyrics copyright 1939 by General Mills, Inc. Used by permission—"Wave the Flag for Hudson High." Lyrics by David Owen and music by Phillip R. Culkin. Copyright 1940 by General Mills, Inc. Used by permission. **103:** Walter Lippmann quotes: New York *Herald Tribune,* April 28, 1932; *Review of Reviews,* May 1933—Will Rogers quotes: *The Autobiography of Will Rogers,* Donald Day, ed., Houghton Mifflin, 1949, pp. 312-313; *How We Elect Our Presidents,* Donald Day, ed., Little, Brown, 1952, pp. 143-144, 148-149. **104:** Fireside Chat: *The Public Papers and Addresses of Franklin D. Roosevelt,* Vol. 2, "The Year of Crisis: 1933," Random House, 1938, pp. 61-65. **145:** "Tutti Frutti," Doris Fisher and Slim Gaillard. Copyright 1938 by Anne-Rachel Music Corporation. Copyright renewed 1965 and assigned to Anne-Rachel Music Corporation and Fred Fisher Music Co., Inc.—"Three Little Fishies," Saxie Dowell. Copyright 1939 by Anne-Rachel Music Corporation. Copyright renewed 1966 and assigned to Anne-Rachel Music Corporation—"The Flat Foot Floogee," Slim Gaillard, Slam Stewart, and Bud Green. © 1938, 1966 Jewel Music Publishing Co., Inc. at 1619 Broadway, N.Y., N.Y. 10019. **151:** Huey Long quotes: Huey P. Long, *My First Days in the White House,* Telegraph Press, Harrisburg, Pa., 1935. **152:** Father Coughlin quotes: *New York Times,* March 4, 1935; July 17, 1936; *Time* magazine, October 5, 1936; *New York Times,* November 21, 1938. **156:** Wilfred Mendelson letters: *Let My People Know,* Joseph Leeds, ed., New York, 1942.

PICTURE CREDITS

The sources for the illustrations in this book are listed below. Credits from left to right are separated by semicolons, from top to bottom by dashes.

Cover and dust jacket: Loraine Burdick; Photo Files; Corbis-Bettmann; Library of Congress; Culver Pictures (3)—photograph by Dorothea Lange, Library of Congress neg. no. F34-9058C.
3: Chicago Tribune-New York News Syndicate, courtesy Woody Gelman. **6, 7:** Library of Congress. **8, 9:** Brown Brothers, Sterling, Pa. **10-13:** Library of Congress. **14, 15:** Edholm and Blomgren, Lincoln, Nebr. **16, 17:** Al P. Burgert. **18, 19:** Culver Pictures, Inc., New York. **20, 21:** Historical Collection Security Pacific National Bank. **22, 23:** Museum of the City of New York. **24:** Courtesy Halbert F. Speer. **30, 31:** Culver Pictures, Inc., New York. **33:** Corbis-Bettmann. **34:** Culver Pictues, Inc., New York. **35:** Culver Pictures, Inc., New York (2); Irving Settel. **36:** CBS Photo Archive, New York. **37, 38:** Culver Pictures, Inc., New York. **40, 41:** University of Washington Library. **43:** Brown Brothers, Sterling, Pa. **44:** *The Detroit News.* **45-47:** Library of Congress. **48, 49:** Margaret Bourke-White; Library of Congress. **50, 51:** Margaret Bourke-White. **52, 53:** Mrs. Henry Rhoades. **54-63:** Library of Congress. **64, 65:** Western Ways Features. **67:** Wayne State University, Labor History Archives. **68:** Chicago Tribune-New York News Syndicate, courtesy Woody Gelman. **69:** Courtesy Ernest Trova, photographed by John Savage. **70:**

Courtesy Al Williamson. **71:** Culver Pictures, Inc., New York—courtesy Douglas Steinbauer, photographed by Al Freni (4), except bottom right, courtesy Woody Gelman and Nostalgia Press. **72:** General Mills, Inc. (2); courtesy Ernest Trova, photographed by John Savage—General Mills, Inc.—General Mills, Inc., photographed by Al Freni. **73:** General Mills, Inc.—General Mills, Inc., photographed by Al Freni—courtesy Ernest Trova, photographed by John Savage (2). **74:** Courtesy United Features Syndicate. **75:** Metro-Goldwyn-Mayer. **76:** Courtesy Ernest Trova, photographed by John Savage, except bottom left courtesy Ernest Trova and Ralston Purina Co. **77:** Courtesy Ernest Trova, photographed by John Savage. **78, 79:** From the Buck Rogers Collection of Tony Goodstone, New York City, photographed by Al Freni. **80, 81:** Courtesy Ernest Trova, photographed by John Savage, except cartoons, courtesy Chicago Tribune-New York News Syndicate, photographed by Walter Daran. **82:** Courtesy Loraine Burdick (2); Marcus Adams, London. **83:** Courtesy Loraine Burdick. **84:** Courtesy Ione Wollenzein, photographed by Al Freni; courtesy Loraine Burdick; courtesy Ione Wollenzein. **85:** Courtesy Ione Wollenzein, photographed by Al Freni. **86, 87:** *Houston Chronicle.* **89:** No credit. **90:** Collection of the Little Bohemia Lodge, Manitowish Waters, Wis. **91:** UPI/Corbis-Bettmann. **92:** *Daily Oklahoman* (2); No credit. **93:** AP/Wide World Photos. **94:** *Daily Oklahoman;* UPI/Corbis-Bettmann (2). **95:** Charles Moore/Black Star. **96:** Brown Brothers, Sterling, Pa. **98, 99:** Tom McAvoy. **100:** Reprinted from *Vanity Fair* copyright © 1934, 1962 by The Condé Nast Publications Inc. **102, 103:** UPI/Corbis-Bettmann. **105:** Reproduced by permission of *Esquire* Magazine © 1935 (renewed 1963) by Esquire, Inc. **106, 107:** Franklin D. Roosevelt Library, Hyde Park, N.Y. **108:** Corbis-Bettmann. **109:** AP/Wide World Photos. **110:** Culver Pictures, Inc., New York—Photo World/FPG International LLC. **111:** Corbis-Bettmann. **112, 113:** From *Public Building* by Public Works Administrations and Federal Works Agency. **114:** Culver Pictures, Inc., New York; National Collection of Fine Arts photographed by Henry B. Beville. **116, 117:** Interphoto. **119:** Harris & Ewing. **120, 121:** Wayne State University, Labor History Archives. **122:** Library of Congress. **123:** AP/Wide World Photos (2)—UPI/Corbis-Bettmann. **124, 125:** Wayne State University, Labor History Archives. **126:** UPI/Corbis-Bettmann—William Vandivert. **127:** UPI/Corbis-Bettmann, except top right, Historical Society of Pennsylvania. **128:** Brown Brothers, Sterling, Pa. **129:** Drawing by William Gropper. **130, 131:** AP/Wide World Photos. **133:** Library of Congress. **134, 135:** Popsie, New York. **137:** Otto F. Hess. **138:** No credit; Ernest R. Smith—Brown Brothers, Sterling, Pa.; Corbis-Bettmann. **139:** *Down Beat* Magazine; Brown Brothers, Sterling, Pa.; Photo Files; Duncan P. Schiedt; Photo Files. **140:** *Down Beat* Magazine; Popsie, New York (2). **141:** Popsie, New York. **142, 143:** Peter Stackpole, *Life* Magazine © Time Inc. **144:** *New York Daily News;* Duncan P. Schiedt—Hansel Meith; Richard Merrill—Ernest R. Smith. **145:** Duncan P. Schiedt—Pete Culross; UPI/Corbis-Bettmann—Photo Files; Bernard Hoffman. **146, 147:** Alfred Eisenstaedt/Pix. **149:** Otto Hagel. **150:** Louisiana State Museum. **153:** AP/Wide World Photos. **154:** Hans Knopf/Pix. **156, 157:** AP/Wide World Photos. **158, 159:** Historical Collection, Title Insurance and Trust Company, San Diego, Calif. **161:** Credits for this page are listed according to amount used from each source: UPI/Corbis-Bettmann; AP/Wide World Photos; Culver Pictures, Inc., New York; Clarence Sinclair Bull-MGM; Paramount Pictures; Ron Partridge/Black Star; 20th Century-Fox; Rex Hardy. **162, 163:** Culver Pictures, Inc., New York. **164:** Collection Herman G. Weinberg. **165:** Corbis-Bettmann. **166:** Culver Pictures, Inc., New York—© 1936 Warner Bros. Pictures, Inc. Ren. 1963 United Artists Associated, Inc. Photo courtesy Photo Files; © 1939 Warner Bros. Pictures, Inc. Ren. 1967 United Artists Television, Inc. Photo courtesy The Academy of Motion Picture Arts and Sciences; © 1939 Warner Bros. Pictures, Inc. Ren. 1967 United Artists Television, Inc. Photo courtesy Culver Pictures, Inc., New York—© 1939 Warner Bros. Pictures, Inc. Ren. 1967 United Artists Television, Inc.; © 1946 Warner Bros. Pictures, Inc. Ren. 1973 United Artists Television, Inc. Photo courtesy Culver Pictures, Inc., New York; © 1937 Warner Bros. Pictures, Inc. Ren. 1964 United Artists

Associated, Inc. Photo courtesy Photo Files. **167:** © 1939 Warner Bros. Pictures, Inc. Ren. 1967 United Artists Television, Inc. **168, 169:** Culver Pictures, Inc., New York. **170, 171:** Brown Brothers, Sterling, Pa. **172-174:** Culver Pictures, Inc., New York. **175:** Culver Pictures, Inc., New York—Metro-Goldwyn-Mayer. **176, 177:** Culver Pictures, Inc., New York. **178, 179:** Walt Disney Productions. **180, 181:** Christie's Images, New York; Movie Still Archives, Harrison, Nebr. **182:** Photofest, New York. **183:** Culver Pictures, Inc., New York, except center, Atlanta Historical Society, Atlanta. **184-187:** Movie Still Archives, Harrison, Nebr.

BIBLIOGRAPHY

American Decades: 1930-1939. Gale Research, 1995.
Amory, Cleveland. *Who Killed Society?* Harper & Row, 1960.
Allen, Frederick Lewis. *Since Yesterday.* Bantam Books, 1965.
Balio, Tino. *Grand Design.* University of California Press, 1993.
Baxter, John. *Hollywood in the Thirties.* A. S. Barnes, 1968.
Bendiner, Robert. *Just Around the Corner.* Harper & Row, 1967.
Bird, Caroline. *The Invisible Scar.* David McKay, 1966.
Blum, Daniel. *A New Pictorial History of the Talkies.* G. P. Putnam's Sons, 1968.
Burns, James MacGregor. *Roosevelt.* Harcourt, Brace, 1956.
Clarens, Carlos. *An Illustrated History of Horror and Science-Fiction Films.* Da Capo Press, 1997.
Coleman, MacAlister. *Men and Coal.* Farrar & Rinehart, 1943.
Cook, Frederick J. *The F.B.I. Nobody Knows.* Macmillan, 1964.
Daniels, Jonathan. *The Time Between the Wars.* Doubleday, 1966.
Feather, Leonard. *The Encyclopedia of Jazz* (rev. ed.). Horizon Press, 1968.
Federal Writers' Project, Works Progress Administration. *These Are Our Lives.* University of North Carolina Press, 1939.
Griffith, Richard, and Arthur Mayer. *The Movies.* Simon & Schuster, 1957.
Gunther, John. *Roosevelt in Retrospect.* Harper & Bros., 1950.
Halliwell, Leslie. *The Filmgoer's Companion.* Hill & Wang, 1967.
Harmon, James. *The Great Radio Heroes.* Ace Books, 1967.
Hoover, J. Edgar. *Persons in Hiding.* Little, Brown, 1938.
Howe, Irving, and Lewis Coser. *The American Communist Party.* Beacon Press, 1957.
Kempton, Murray. *Part of Our Time.* Dell Publishing, 1955.
Leonard, Jonathan Norton. *Three Years Down.* Carrick & Evans, 1939.
Leuchtenburg, William E. *Franklin D. Roosevelt and the New Deal.* Harper & Row, 1963.
Levinson, Edward. *Labor on the March.* Harper & Bros., 1938.
Maxwell, Elsa. *R.S.V.P.* Little, Brown, 1954.
Meltzer, Milton. *Brother Can You Spare a Dime?* Alfred A. Knopf, 1969.
O'Connor, Harvey. *Steel-Dictator.* John Day, 1935.
Roosevelt, James, and Sidney Shalett. *Affectionately, F.D.R.* Harcourt, Brace, 1959.
Schickel, Richard. *The Disney Version.* Simon & Schuster, 1968.
Schlesinger, Arthur M., Jr. *The Age of Roosevelt:*
    The Coming of the New Deal (Vol. 2). Houghton Mifflin, 1958.
    The Politics of Upheaval (Vol 3). Houghton Mifflin, 1960.
Settel, Irving. *A Pictorial History of Radio.* Grosset & Dunlap, 1967.
Simon, George T. *The Big Bands.* Macmillan, 1967.
Sklar, Robert. *Movie-Made America.* Vintage Books, 1994.
Taft, Philip. *Organized Labor in American History.* Harper & Row, 1964.
Tanner, Louise. *All the Things We Were.* Doubleday, 1968.
Taylor, Deems. *A Pictorial History of the Movies.* Simon & Schuster, 1949.
Wecter, Dixon. *The Age of the Great Depression.* Macmillan, 1948.
Whitehead, Donald. *The F.B.I. Story.* Random House, 1956.

INDEX

TIME® LIFE BOOKS

Time-Life Books is a division of Time Life Inc.

TIME LIFE INC.
PRESIDENT and CEO: George Artandi

TIME-LIFE BOOKS
PRESIDENT: Stephen R. Frary
PUBLISHER/MANAGING EDITOR: Neil Kagan
VICE PRESIDENT, MARKETING: Joseph A. Kuna

OUR AMERICAN CENTURY
Hard Times: The 30s

EDITORS: Loretta Britten, Sarah Brash
DIRECTOR, NEW PRODUCT DEVELOPMENT:
Elizabeth D. Ward
DIRECTOR OF MARKETING:
Pamela R. Farrell

Deputy Editor: Charles J. Hagner
Associate Editor/Research and Writing: Samantha Fields
Senior Copyeditor: Anne Farr
Picture Coordinator: Betty H. Weatherley
Editorial Assistant: Christine Higgins

Design for **Our American Century** by Antonio Alcalá, Studio A, Alexandria, Virginia.

Special Contributors: Maggie Debelius, Philip Brandt George, Paul Mathless (text); Kimberly Grandcolas (production); Richard Friend, Christina Hagopian (design); Susan Nedrow (index).

Correspondents: Maria Vincenza Aloisi (Paris), Christine Hinze (London), Christina Lieberman (New York).

Director of Finance: Christopher Hearing
Directors of Book Production: Marjann Caldwell, Patricia Pascale
Director of Publishing Technology: Betsi McGrath
Director of Photography and Research: John Conrad Weiser
Director of Editorial Administration: Barbara Levitt
Production Manager: Gertraude Schaefer
Quality Assurance Manager: James King
Chief Librarian: Louise D. Forstall

This revised edition was originally published as
THIS FABULOUS CENTURY: 1930-1940.

EDITORIAL CONSULTANT
Richard B. Stolley is currently senior editorial adviser at Time Inc. After 19 years at *Life* magazine as a reporter, bureau chief, and assistant managing editor, he became the first managing editor of *People* magazine, a position he held with great success for eight years. He then returned to *Life* magazine as managing editor and later served as editorial director for all Time Inc. magazines. In 1997 Stolley received the Henry Johnson Fisher Award for Lifetime Achievement, the magazine industry's highest honor.

Library of Congress Cataloging-in-Publication Data
Hard times, the 30s / by the editors of Time-Life Books.
p. cm.—(Our American century)
Includes bibliographical references (p.   ) and index.
ISBN 0-7835-5505-9
1. Nineteen thirties. 2. Nineteen thirties—Pictorial works.
3. United States—History—1933-1945. 4. United States—History—1933-1945—Pictorial works. 5. Depressions—1929—United States. 6. Depressions—1929—United States—Pictorial works. 7. New Deal, 1933-1939. 8. New Deal, 1933-1939—Pictorial works.
I. Time-Life Books. II. Series.
E806.H325   1998
973.917—dc21   98-21924
                                                         CIP

Other History Publications:

World War II
What Life Was Like
The American Story
Voices of the Civil War
The American Indians
Lost Civilizations
Mysteries of the Unknown
Time Frame
The Civil War
Cultural Atlas

For information on and a full description of any of the Time-Life Books series listed above, please call 1-800-621-7026 or write:

Reader Information
Time-Life Customer Service
P.O. Box C-32068
Richmond, Virginia 23261-2068